ADVANCE PRAISE

"*High achievers are often negatively influenced by unhealthy and unproductive drivers. Ted Bradshaw shows a different way: it's better to be guided than driven. Laying out a clear framework to follow, Bradshaw provides practical tools to use to support the journey to living to your highest potential.*"

—DAN SULLIVAN, CO-FOUNDER &
PRESIDENT OF STRATEGIC COACH®

"*Ted Bradshaw understands high achievers. His valuable insights and examples found in this book help them to uncover the life they were meant to live and the instruction manual on how to live it.*"

—GINO WICKMAN, BESTSELLING AUTHOR
OF *TRACTION* AND *THE EOS LIFE*

"*In Stop Chasing Squirrels, Ted offers a fresh approach to the eternal question of why we are here and how best to spend our time while we are. A must-read for anyone looking to find meaning and direction in their lives.*"

—STEVE STAIOS, FORMER NATIONAL HOCKEY
LEAGUE PLAYER & WORLD CHAMPION

STOP CHASING SQUIRRELS

6 Essentials to Find Your
Purpose, Focus, and Flow

STOP

CHASING

SQUIRRELS

TED BRADSHAW

FOREWORD BY GINO WICKMAN

LIONCREST
PUBLISHING

STOP CHASING SQUIRRELS
6 Essentials to Find Your Purpose, Focus, and Flow

FIRST EDITION

ISBN   978-1-5445-3157-1 *Hardcover*
          978-1-5445-3158-8 *Paperback*
          978-1-5445-3159-5 *Ebook*
          978-1-5445-3160-1 *Audiobook*

To my beautiful wife, Jennifer. You are my rock, my soulmate, and your unconditional love and support continue to give me the courage to follow my purpose. And also to my son, Spencer, and my daughter, Kirsten. I am so proud of you both and love you more than words convey. You inspire me every day to be the best version of myself.

CONTENTS

FOREWORD BY GINO WICKMAN

BESTSELLING AUTHOR OF
TRACTION AND *THE EOS LIFE*

I first met Ted Bradshaw in 2016, when he joined the EOS community as a Professional EOS Implementer. EOS stands for Entrepreneurial Operating System, a practical method of achieving business success. Our community is a gathering of leaders who help business owners get what they want from their businesses. The culture of the EOS community is defined by our core values, which we hold dear.

When our paths crossed, I knew immediately Ted was all about those values. He has that rare combination of big-picture vision and small-picture know-how. Not only that, but he's a born communicator. In no time, he became a key player in our community.

For the first ten years of building EOS Worldwide, I facilitated our quarterly meetings in Detroit for the global implementer community. This included training incredible people to become EOS Implementers. As we expanded geographically, Ted became the first EOS Implementer to facilitate quarterly meetings in Denver and train people to become Professional EOS Implementers.

Now, I've asked him to succeed me in leading Freedom Forum, which helps our best implementers protect what they've earned and ultimately live what we fondly call the EOS Life. And what's the EOS Life? Five things:

→ Doing what you love
→ With people you love
→ Making a huge difference
→ Being compensated appropriately
→ With time for other passions

Ted and I agree that everybody deserves to live their ideal life. We also agree that most entrepreneurs are falling short of that. I wrote *Traction* and *The EOS Life* to address this problem. And now Ted is bringing us brand new insights, based on what he calls the life guided by purpose. Ted is all about helping you get the most from your life while having the time of your life.

His passion is highly contagious, so watch out. As you read this book, I believe your passion for life will receive a powerful jolt. Ted practices what he preaches, and everything he teaches is proven. He's found his way toward his ideal life, and he can show you how to get there, too. Ted wrote this book with a passion and a purpose, and that purpose is to help you find yours.

In his twenty-five years as an entrepreneur and hundreds of sessions working with team leaders, he's found what I did: that good leaders can become disillusioned, disconnected, and dislocated. They find themselves "chasing squirrels"—launching out toward any distraction that offers a small taste of the joy they're missing in their daily work.

There's one cure for that, Ted says: the discovery and pursuit of true purpose. But he offers no neat formulas to get that item checked off your list with next week's responsibilities. It's going to take a life of dedication to purpose, and here you'll find out how to do that, too.

This is a must-read for every leader who feels he or she is simply missing something that he or she knows in his or her soul should be there. If you're interested in finding why you were placed on this planet and what you're supposed to do about it, buckle your seat belt. You're about to begin a journey of discovering those answers—and like all journeys, it will transform you along the way.

INTRODUCTION

"If you chase two rabbits, you catch none."

—CONFUCIUS

I work with high achievers. No, not on the Jeff Bezos level—not that high—but still, people who get things done. They're visionary, creative, and entrepreneurial. And most of them have already enjoyed their share of career success.

These aren't people who you'd catch sleeping late or daydreaming the afternoon away. They're hard-charging, they're fully engaged with their work, and still, they go to bed at night with brand-new ideas dancing around in their heads. It's hard for them to turn off that flow and get to sleep sometimes. Creative energy has no off switch. Have you ever noticed that?

People like that are primed that way. They're naturally, instinctively on the lookout for new concepts, new possibilities, and whatever might be around the next bend in the road. So they go through life, day to day, and every stray thought is a variation on the theme of what if. The tantalizing ideas leap out at the oddest times: at restaurants, during yard work, in church or synagogue, and, of course, at one in the morning.

Sometimes they tell me, "I get twenty new ideas a week—twenty big ideas; nineteen of them probably aren't very good. But one of them, just one of them, might be the brilliant concept that sends my company to the moon. Know what I mean?"

I do.

But then these friends pause for a second, sigh, and admit, "Or maybe I'm just chasing squirrels."

Have you ever seen how dogs chase squirrels? One pops up, just over the hedge. Fido takes off after it, but the squirrel is already up the tree—and look! Another squirrel!

Creative, energetic people can be like that. There's an idea, a glimmer of one tiny corner of a possibility. A could-be, a how-about. And they're hot in pursuit. Every now and then creative people become discouraged by the whole thing.

Because that same pattern plays out not just with ideas, but in everyday life. They chase after this exercise program, that trendy diet, the other new hobby, or the latest get-rich-quick scheme. Then one day, Facebook sends them one of those "memory" notifications: this was you, five years ago.

And they think, *Look at the squirrel I was chasing. That exercise program. That diet. That hobby. How many since then?*

There's a lot of that going around. We are, after all, the ADHD generation. Information is almost too accessible. The internet makes it possible to chase countless squirrels in infinite directions. Maybe we need to look away, give it a rest, unplug for a while.

Or maybe it's a touch of what I came down with, years ago: a bad case of drivenness. Of moving in every direction, without a map.

When I was a young businessman, chasing possibilities didn't seem like a bug, but a feature. I was wide open, pedal to the floor, going after new business ideas and quickly shifting directions like a hockey player skating down the ice with the time about to expire. Which, by the way, was part of my identity back in the day.

I was an entrepreneur. One of these directions, or maybe several of them, would hit pay dirt. It didn't particularly matter to me which of them did. That was my idea of what an entrepreneur is—someone who sees openings, grabs them, monetizes them, then moves on to the next big thing.

I was in Xerox management in the mid-nineties, and I did well. I realized I had a clear career path in a large corporation, with plenty of room for advancement. After a few years, I moved to IBM, and again, I found the fast track. But I knew I wanted more than to be a cog in a large machine. I wanted my own business. I wanted to work with intellectual properties that I owned, rather than those owned by Fortune 500 companies. My desire was to run the machine rather than be a cog in it.

This was the nineties, the dot-com bubble had yet to burst, and I knew it was the time to move into technology. My partners and I created software to connect K–12 schools with homes, just as people were beginning to bring the internet into their households.

We were very successful. I was hearing about how we were helping the students, their parents, and the schools.

That was fine; it made me feel good. But my drive was purely in the business direction. It didn't matter so much whether or not I was doing something virtuous; I wanted to create enterprise, make profits, and move on to other startups.

As a matter of fact, in the midst of that, while at a software trade show, I heard about a company that developed virtual world *games* for kids. They sold their platform to Disney for $700 million. I caught my breath when I heard those numbers. We were doing well with school software, but not to the tune of three quarters of a billion.

This was like building a fine, comfortable house, being proud of it, then seeing a megamansion move into the neighborhood. I'd been thinking too small! The lesson was clear: entertainment trumps education in the world of profit. My outlook was to go big or go home. So we got out of the education business and quickly moved into developing a video game company built around hockey— again, one of my great loves. We partnered with the National Hockey League.

All this time I had a wonderful family, a great home (though no megamansion), and if you'd been watching, you'd have seen me as I saw myself: a driven guy on his way up. But it was about this time that I hit my biggest bump in the road as an entrepreneur.

Just a bit too late, we discovered that the major trend in the gaming industry was going mobile. PC screens, where our hockey game was played, were no longer the cool thing. Games were moving to Facebook and cell phones. We'd been beaten to the next market—victims of Angry Birds!

Anyone can play the role of "nice guy on his way up." But what happens when the nice guy finally stumbles? When his business idea fizzles—and the next one, too? When tensions develop with your team? I handled things the best way I knew how, and moved on.

But now I found the way forward to be far rockier. I knew I wasn't infallible, for one thing. All I knew was to keep pressing forward, to double down on my hours and my determination, and to make the next idea a success through sheer force of will. In hockey, when you get knocked down, you recover as quickly as you can and get back into the play. You're just a little bruised and a little angrier now.

I finally came to a crisis point. I experienced a couple of panic attacks, seemingly out of nowhere. My inner life was in chaos, yet somehow I was the last to know—my body got the message to me through these two terrible experiences that felt like heart attacks: one in the middle of a busy airport, once while driving my son to hockey practice.

In both cases, the doctors and emergency techs told me there was absolutely nothing wrong with my health. These moments were "straws that broke the camel's back." Stress piled on top of stress until the result was a panic attack. And when I didn't fix things, another panic attack.

Needless to say, though, my family was shaken and so was I. It was time to take stock of my life. And for the next several years, I began sorting it all out. Who was I, really? What was wrong with what I was doing, and how could I make things right? I reflected more than I ever had, and for the first time, got to know a little bit about this guy Ted Bradshaw.

What I discovered is that we chase squirrels when we lack purpose, that we can only keep chasing for so long until we drop with exhaustion or become miserable with frustration, that this is no way to live.

In the process of all this, thankfully, I also discovered exactly why I was placed on this earth. When I coach, when I help others, it lights me up inside. It gives me joy like nothing else. There are many things I'm not very good at, but I'm good with people, and good with coaching. When I'm doing what I love, it's actually the precise opposite of those terrible moments I had when I lacked focus and was running businesses that made me miserable and left me unfulfilled. Instead of going dark inside, what I do now brightens my soul. My relationships are better. My health is better. And, of course, I'm more successful in the work I do, because it's the work I love to do and that I excel at doing.

This book lays out the essence of these discoveries, in a way that you can make use of them, too. Here, in brief, is the world we'll be exploring together in this book.

First, we'll begin where we must begin: in the chaos that too many of us experience when we're not guided by purpose but driven by other things. We'll see just what those other things are—negative emotions that are terribly destructive. I speak from experience here, and you may see yourself in that chapter, too. But it shouldn't be a negative experience. We'll discover that there are simply some emotions and valleys of life we have to struggle through if we're going to reach the greener hills we're heading for. By understanding these negative drivers, we can finally be freed from bondage to them. And the next time they threaten to move in, we'll recognize them and know how to defeat them.

Second, we'll talk about you—where you are right now. I'll talk you through a personal assessment exercise that will help you evaluate who you are, where your best skills lie, what makes you happiest, and hopefully, what kind of focus that suggests for your life. I've done this with many people, and it's the most exciting experience I can imagine. This could be a moment of supreme self-realization for you, and it may reroute your direction to an alternate path that you'll wish you'd discovered long ago.

Then, we'll take up a key concept in this idea of life focus. It's the concept of a long, straight path in a dedicated direction for the duration of your life. When you hear someone talking about solving your problems in one week, or losing this weight or finding instant success through this quick formula, you're looking at a mirage. None of that is offered here. Purpose may be revealed in a day, a week, a moment. It could certainly be uncovered in the reading of this book.

But moving toward it is the journey of life itself. There are no shortcuts. So we'll talk about six essential elements—basics of life, really—that will keep you on that path, and what you can do to maintain them as the years go on. I find that many people work on one or two of these. But when you realize the significance of all six, and nurture them all, the results are electrifying.

From there, all that follows is to go into greater depth on each of these essentials: the mind, the body, the soul, nutrition, money, and relationships. Each chapter will bring you surprises as you find new ways of understanding who you are, why you do the things you do, and who you could be.

As I've said, I work with high achievers. Some of them are tired of chasing squirrels. More and more, they're realizing the rock-solid truth of what Curly (Jack Palance) tells Billy Crystal's character, Mitch, in the 1991 movie *City Slickers*. Mitch asks him, in a rather condescending manner, "Do you know what the secret of life is?"

Curly holds up one finger.

Rolling his eyes, Mitch says, "Your finger?"

Curly says, "One thing. Just one thing. You stick to that and the rest don't mean shit."

Mitch asks him what the one thing is, and Curly smiles and replies, "That's what you have to find out."

Find one thing, and stick to it. I think Curly just wrote our book. But do you know what your one thing is?

Let's begin the adventure of finding out.

CHAPTER ONE

WHY WE CHASE SQUIRRELS

"People who labor all their lives but have no purpose to direct every thought and impulse toward are wasting their time—even when hard at work."

—MARCUS AURELIUS

Show me a high achiever, and I'll show you someone who sets goals. I've always been that way; I need something out in front of me that's just beyond my grasp. It keeps my adrenaline going, gets me up a little earlier in the morning, and focuses me in the right direction.

Something else I've noticed: there comes a moment when reaching one more goal doesn't bring the same thrill. I got this done, and that's great. I got this next thing done, hooray! But after a while, a lot of us come to that moment when we suddenly wonder, is this all there is? How many goals, how many victories, push me across the line that finally makes me feel successful?

I've come to believe that genuine satisfaction—the kind we can feel deep inside, and in a lasting way—transcends any and all of our transient goals. You can be the highest achiever in your field, you can outwork and outearn every competitor, and still, you might have that feeling that something's missing if there isn't a deeper purpose giving meaning to the whole journey.

In the previous pages, I described my own journey. Over time, and through facing up to certain hard truths for the first time, I came to realize I was a driven individual. The panic attacks were my body getting an urgent message through to my heart and soul: this path wasn't sustainable. It was killing me. It was sabotaging important relationships.

I didn't want to be driven anymore. I did a lot of thinking about the right word, the one that described what I did want—and I came up with this one: *guided*.

THE DRIVEN LIFE

If you google the word "driven," you'll find a lot of information about the habits of highly motivated individuals. Being driven is generally presented as a positive thing, the description of those who have a high energy to get things done. *Driven* is one of those ambiguous words that can be used positively or negatively—like the word *pride*, for example. It's good to be proud of our children, or to take pride in our work. Yet pride is also listed as a sin! It's all about the nature of the pride, isn't it?

Drivenness is similar. It's a positive or a negative depending on the driver. We do tend to think of highly driven people in a good way. They have a will to succeed, and what could be wrong with that? They're workers. They're achievers.

The problem comes in *how* and *why* they might be motivated. Not every goal or source of emotional drive is a healthy one. Some driver is pushing us to our limits in order to get certain things done. It could be a sense of competition. We have to outdo that competitor, right? Or it could be some need to prove ourselves, or live up to someone's expectations.

Most of us have observed people who are unhealthily driven. I'd be highly surprised if this book didn't fall into the hands of people who have been there themselves. Buying this very book could be the result of being driven. So it's worth thinking about what's behind all that motivation.

Those who are driven feel a pressure from somewhere to do more— and better—and faster. If you were to sit them down and ask, "What's driving you?" you might not get a quick answer. There is no *why* within easy reach. They may never have even given the source of motivation a thought. They just know they're in a hurry to some level of achievement. There is a drive that may be invisible to them, and somehow, that drive never goes away. There's never the feeling of, "Well, that's satisfying. I did it!" Perhaps for a few minutes or a few days, it's possible to experience a sense of accomplishment. But then the driven person starts feeling that pressure again.

Many driven people don't rest well. They don't care for their health as they should. Nor do they give enough thought to the people around them who are pulled along by this unrelenting course of rugged effort. Eventually, those with an unhealthy drive tend to burn out. They come to that point at which it's suddenly clear the goalposts are going to keep moving and the finish line will keep edging toward the horizon. Then something just cracks. They can't do it anymore.

Being *driven* is letting the wind blow our boat every which way. It's being powered and directed by that merciless outside gust of wind. When we're driven, it feels, at first, as if we're going somewhere; we're on the move, maybe even *fast*. The adrenaline feels good. There's a little dopamine surge of pleasure: "Let's go!" There are others who actually feed off your energy, because you're a real go-getter.

But the hidden truth is that you're not the one setting the direction. In the end, you end up way off course. Lost. Confused.

Nature abhors a vacuum, so if we don't take control, something else will. And somehow, it's never anything good. Why is that? Wouldn't it be wonderful if a spirit of goodwill, benevolence, and philanthropy just washed over people sometimes, as if they were catching a good kind of virus? "Have you heard? Ed caught that virtue bug that's going around. He's running around buying gifts, doing nice things for everybody in town!"

Human nature doesn't work that way, unfortunately. Misplaced and unhealthy emotions creep in without us realizing it. They gently relieve us of the oars and begin guiding the vessel. It always *feels* as if we're the captain of our ship; we tell ourselves, hey, we've got this. But the truth is, it's got *us*.

It's a rough day indeed once we figure it out. I speak from personal experience, as I've explained. Once I hit the wall, stopped, and took inventory of how things really were in my life, I decided I wanted no more of the driven life. But what was the option?

I asked myself how I like to be treated when I'm going places. There might be some meeting I need to go to, but I'm not too excited about it. You could get me there, I suppose, by threatening me. You could use a high-pressure sales approach. You could try frightening me into going, because of what I might miss. Maybe you'd be successful, but I don't really do well with that kind of pressure. I don't know many people who do. I'd rather someone reason with me, tell me why the meeting's important, and give me good, solid encouragement that I should go because it's a very worthy meeting and I'll love what happens there.

In other words, I don't want to be driven. I want to be guided.

THE GUIDED LIFE

Let's go sailing again.

We talked about being driven by ill winds. The idea is that we're going somewhere, but we're being controlled by outside forces. That's being driven. Being *guided* is taking the initiative to bring a map—to adjust the sail and the rudder, to take up the oars, and to direct the vessel to a destination you've carefully chosen.

Driven people tend to be unaware of the drivers. They're slaves to unknown masters. But guided people decide their own direction. And what guides them? A sense of purpose. It's possible, of course, to be guided by an unworthy purpose. You might be planning to rob a bank, and you might take a thoughtful, well-organized, efficient course toward a successful robbery. Obviously, that's not what we're describing. We all know there are healthy, worthy purposes. I believe everyone in the world has a purpose, and it's just the right fit for who we are—our talents, our temperaments, our values, and everything else about us. Finding and moving toward that ideal purpose is the surest formula for happiness and contentment. It's the exchange of my life and time for that which brings me the greatest joy and also makes the most positive difference in this world.

In my case, I found that I wasn't on that path. My purpose was not to create x number of new businesses or make y dollars in profit. It was not to build a kingdom dedicated to my sense of ambition.

I know I've found my purpose for life. I'm guided by a deep and abiding passion for helping other people find *their* own unique purpose. It wasn't about me after all, in one sense, but about inspiring others. Yet ironically, because I've chosen this path and geared it to my gifts, it's actually a lot *more* about me than when I believed it was *all* about me. If that makes sense! The point is, I'm personally the happiest when I'm invested in the happiness of others. I know exactly what I want to do and how I want to do it, and each day is another mile in that direction.

Goals? They're still there, but they look and feel different. My life is organized in a disciplined and orderly way around shorter- and longer-term goals that are thoughtfully based on my life focus.

This book is actually one more part of my life purpose, which is to help you find yours. But in the next chapter, we'll discuss that period I've been describing, when the boat seems to be tossed about. We can't skip over it, because that's where the journey really begins. You may be there right now. So let's talk about the "ill winds" that blow us off course.

One recommendation: if you do see yourself in this chapter, there's no reason to be discouraged. All of this is fuel. These tougher times are the ones that help us grow the most. I'd never be where I am now if I hadn't struggled through my own crises. I had to see what it was like and how it felt to lead a purposeless life.

YOUR TIMELINE

In this book, we'll look toward a focused life of purpose. We'll get there by talking about our past—particularly what we want to leave in the past—our present, and that future we're driving toward. Here's a simplified structure for the next couple of chapters:

PAST	6 Drivers	Recognizing our lack of control, and moving from driven to guided.
PRESENT	Temperature Check	Recognizing who we are in order to begin the discovery of what we should be doing.
FUTURE	Getting to Why	Realizing how to create the life we deeply desire.

So let's think about the time of your life—all your life: where you've been, and where you want to go. I'm certainly not the first writer to observe that life is a journey. We'll be drawing on that metaphor consistently to help us conceptualize the big ideas here. How do you prepare for an important road trip?

I enjoy hiking, so I tend to think about preparing for a long walk down a wilderness path, with the beauty of nature all around me.

I'm sure you've done at least a little hiking. So imagine reading this book, then taking all your "takeaways" from these pages and packing them carefully into a backpack, as you first set out on your walk. These takeaways will be parts of who you are: your interests, talents, experiences, goals, values, and so on. You can't go anywhere without them.

Now you try on your backpack, and it's pretty hefty. We can carry a lot on our backs. But you'll be exhausted after each day's hike. Life is like that when we carry a lot on our shoulders.

Maybe you don't need everything in the pack. Believe me, I've gone through this process when packing for a trip. Can I get down to one suitcase? Do I really need to take this many clothes?

That's what you're thinking, so you go through your pack again and immediately see a couple of items that really don't need to be a part of this journey. Remember the kind of journey we're talking about: a life of focused purpose, your best life. Go ahead and pull those unnecessary items out. Your back muscles will be grateful.

And so, you set out and begin the journey, you and your values, goals, talents, interests, and dreams. But in time, you realize a few more of those items seem less essential. They just don't seem important anymore. You lay these aside, and your pack is smaller again and lighter.

What you're doing is cutting away those time and energy consumers that don't contribute to the purpose you're now all about, because with each passing day of this hike, you have a tighter focus on what that purpose is, and you're also more committed to it.

Eventually your backpack is almost empty—nothing in there but what really counts. You hardly even *need* a backpack anymore, because your purpose is tight and concentrated. Once you realize that, you discard the backpack itself and place that purpose in your front pocket, the one close to your heart, where all true life purposes reside. And onward you move, traveling light and quickly.

We begin with the past, but remember—the past leads right up to this moment, when it becomes the present. It's likely that some of these drivers are part of you right now. We discuss them in past terms, however, because that's exactly where we want to leave them. Let's go through your backpack, figure out what they are, and leave them by the side of the trail so you can be guided by a strong sense of purpose, rather than driven by the wrong elements.

CHAPTER TWO

WHAT DRIVES US

"Knowing yourself is the beginning of all wisdom."

—ARISTOTLE

Have you ever been a relentless, driven person—or is it possible you could still be one? Don't answer without giving it some careful thought.

If you've been driven—what controls you? It could be an emotion, a powerful desire, a basic drive, or even the influence of someone else. You can be controlled by fear. You can be controlled by drugs or alcohol or appetite, by shame or greed, by religious dogma or legal contract.

Most of us want to believe we've got it all in hand. But do we really? It takes a serious, comprehensive look at our time, our schedule, and how we spend our money to get the best clues about what stimulates our actions.

Think of the beautiful lives projected in social media. We want to be like these people, so we let those images (usually airbrushed, polished, and deceptive ones) drive us. Or we might be driven by some conception in our head—what Dad used to stand for, what Steve Jobs achieved, or what the person next door is getting done.

Nor does it have to be one particular thing. Have you ever felt driven by conflicting voices wanting you to go in different directions? Think of the teenager who's strongly motivated, for the first time in her life, by the voices of peers—all the while hearing a very different set of directives from parents whom she loves. Life itself is learning to choose which directives among many to follow.

But I believe there are certain basic human emotions that are powerful, universal, and the most likely forces to take control if we're not steering our own ships. I've identified six different drives that I believe motivate those of us who lack purpose.

I've experienced each one of these; I'm betting you have, too. They're basic human feelings that come and go in life. But when they push forward and begin to control us, we experience chaos.

JEALOUSY

Jealousy and envy are two similar emotions. Envy is a bit simpler. It's seeing what someone else has and wanting it. A friend has a shiny new Ferrari and you think, *Boy, I wish that were mine.* You might even tell your friend you envy his car; he'll take it as a compliment.

Jealousy is envy that makes it personal. It thinks in terms of rivalries. It's more like, "You have what should be mine." A little envy could be harmless, but jealousy is never healthy. Not only do you desperately want what they have, but you justify it by filling your mind with negative thoughts about the person who has it.

When you're jealous, you see someone's words and actions in a dark light. "What a fake," you think. "Life isn't fair, or I'd be where this guy is. I'd have what he has." As we'll see, there are connections here to resentment, to materialism, and to guilt, all of which are emotional drivers we'll discuss. "I'm jealous of what you have," you think, "so I resent you for having it, and now I feel guilty for these feelings of resentment." These drivers overlap.

If you've struggled with jealousy, a name or a face may come to mind. Is there anyone in particular that brings out these negative emotions in you? How did you begin experiencing these feelings? How do these feelings affect your spirit and attitude?

What if you had a powerful, focused sense of purpose—a purpose that was yours alone, custom-fit to your personality and sense of satisfaction? You'd be much less likely to think in terms of rivalries and what the other person is doing, because your own sense of mission would be so well-defined. Purpose-guided people compete only with themselves, and they stay too busy doing that to brood over jealousy.

GUILT

Guilt is another word for dwelling on history. The past has a hold on us, and we can't break free.

Like anger, like fear, like so many emotions, guilt can actually serve a good purpose, within limits. The conscience is telling us we're better than this, that we've acted beneath our standards of behavior. None of us want to feel bad about ourselves, so in its most productive form, guilt is a built-in defense mechanism to keep us on the straight path.

But guilt is notable for taking on a life of its own, for overstepping its bounds. Guilt offers pain with no remedy. We all have our bad moments, but guilt alone prevents us from feeling forgiven or absolved. If we've actually wronged someone, we can always make amends. We can be inspired to be better people.

But the real problem is often false guilt. It's possible to feel guilty for no valid reason at all.

How? We pick up certain ideas. Parents can place a lot of those in the minds of their children. "You'll never amount to anything." "We've given you every advantage, and you've done nothing but disappoint us." Other life events can leave emotional debris as well. Have you ever had a friend who carried a toxic burden of guilt? No matter how much you tell them to stop beating themselves up, the guilt seems real to them because it feels real.

It's very difficult to break free of an idea repeated by Mom or Dad over and over until it creates a little recording that keeps playing in the head. Long after our parents or mentors have left the earth, their words and opinions still cast their shadow over us.

There are high achievers who constantly spin their wheels out of a sense of unworthiness. They punish themselves through over-work, through trying to prove their value with new achievements. Somehow or other, they'll prove that Dad or the boss or an older brother was wrong about them—only they never seem to get there.

Guilt also sets up a feedback loop. You've probably attended some public function when a microphone and a speaker got in each other's paths and created an awful squeal. It's painful to the ears. Speakers amplify the mic signal, and then the mic, in turn, hears and broadcasts the sound from the speakers—then it escalates to cacophony. Ultimately, the system overloads and the speaker is blown. Guilt bounces back and forth within our heads and does the same kind of damage.

The past belongs right back where you left it—in the past. But if it's feeding back into your current thoughts, it causes interference that becomes very unpleasant, becoming louder and louder. In the end, it can ruin your life, even as an expensive amplifier can be reduced to a useless box with wiring.

Too many people don't even realize they're being driven by simple guilt. The recordings never stop playing, never stop feeding into everything you're trying to do in your present life. It's a driver that can take control, if you let it.

RESENTMENT

Guilt says, "I wronged someone."

Resentment says, "Someone wronged me."

Who knows which is worse? Both have the wrong focus, with the greatest damage done by the imagination. Again, if we're not in control of our thoughts, something else will be. The imagination loves to create. It can take us to some dark places.

Maybe you think back to that promotion your coworker got

instead of you. You're certain you deserved it! And if only you'd gotten that promotion, where would you be now? You'd be on top; you wouldn't have any of these problems that are plaguing you now. That's why you feel all this anxiety: "somebody done somebody wrong." So you either blame yourself (guilt) or you blame someone else (resentment).

Sometimes it's just a general sense of resentment. I played hockey, but I never made it to the NHL. I was the fifth overall draft pick to play junior hockey in the WHL, which is the equivalent of minor-league baseball; the next step is the big time. So if I hadn't gotten busy with other things, I could have dwelt on that and thought about all the people who didn't help me get an agent or the best trainers. I could have nurtured a general sense of resentment: "they" let me down. Who knows, I could have been the next Gretzky! (As I said, the imagination is boundlessly creative.)

Even if there isn't anyone in your current circle to blame, the feelings of resentment can create a negative, bitter mindset. Bitterness itself deserves a mention here, too. In the American South, there's a vine called kudzu that was brought over from Japan in 1876. It's taken over the highways, climbing from tree to tree, and is nearly impossible to remove. Kudzu smothers and kills growing things by blocking out sunlight. It's said of kudzu that "the first year it sleeps. The second year it creeps. The third year it leaps."

Bitterness and resentment are similar; parasitic vines that grow inside our thoughts. If we don't stop them early, they end up blocking out the light and ruining us.

I hear the smallest traces of this emotion when high achievers and entrepreneurs say, "If you want to get me to do something, just tell me I can't!" It sounds positive, gung ho. We're seeking someone to prove wrong, to play the bad guy. Frankly, this is not the most positive mental approach. We need healthier motives, motivation that doesn't require a villain.

The worst situation, of course, is to be resentful of people within our circle. It could be a family member or a coworker. We begin to resent them for real or imagined slights, and the feelings fester until relationships are damaged. Our bitterness invites *their* bitterness, right back at us. We can only handle it one of two ways: we can shut down, be nonconfrontational, and simmer within, possibly exploding later; or we can be confrontational and have the meltdown right up front.

Most people choose to shut down, to bottle up their feelings. The pressure then builds and builds. The anger seeps out in passive-aggressive ways now and then, and the other party figures out there are some negative feelings. Eventually it all comes out, and the confrontation is worse, because again, the imagination has been stoking the fire all this time. Resentment has given way to full-fledged anger.

Another emotion, regret, is often the result. *Where did that come from? How did I let that happen? Did I make things much worse than they were?* In this way we destroy families, businesses, friendships, and many other situations where we interact with people.

The only way to deal with resentment and anger is to let go. *Entirely.* No, it's not easy. Letting go requires a conscious decision, sustained effort, and mental and emotional discipline. But the truth is that emotions can't hurt us unless we maintain and nurture them.

FEAR

Fear is good, right up until it's not.

It's good to fear lightning and to go inside when you see it striking nearby. It's good to fear Crawler's Ledge on the NaPali Coast of Kauai (YouTube it). There are thousands of little things we do out of an appropriate, reality-based fear.

But once again, the imagination is not only an amplifier but a distortion device. If you burned your fingers on a hot stove, the appropriate response would be to avoid touching it in the future when it is hot. The inappropriate response would be to avoid stoves altogether. That would represent an amplified and distorted fear.

It may sound silly, but many people make decisions on that very basis. Psychologists tell us that a great many of our fears and dislikes are irrational. Why do you hate spiders? Is there a rational reason, given that most of them are harmless—or did you have an early experience with spiders that left a mark?

A high achiever obviously can't be ruled by fear. There will be too many occasions that demand some form of courage: making an investment that involves risk, competing with others, simply the fear of failure. But it can happen to those who have a terrible experience, who see a business fail or find themselves having to lay off people they care about who work for them.

Again, a tough lesson might lead to some appropriate fear, but it shouldn't be allowed to dominate us and to overstep its rightful bounds. I've known executives to avoid important decisions entirely because of a bad business experience. In most cases, the issue at hand only festered while it was being ignored, reemerging with a vengeance. Or maybe they were procrastinating, for a fear of repeating a pain that was only connected to a unique situation. The important thing is to act on reason and good sense rather than take counsel of our fears.

What about the worlds of love and passion? Someone falls in love, marries, and then goes through a terribly painful divorce. Soon she's telling friends, "All men are terrible!" And she's half-serious about that. She has opportunities to begin new relationships, but always finds some way to keep her distance, because of the fear of being hurt again. It's a common scenario.

What does fear-based living lead to? We take refuge in our comfort zone, lock the door, and throw away the key. Self-imprisonment: what a sad way to live.

I'll only point out for now that purpose-guided living involves doing what we do best, and working toward the purpose we were designed for. Fear is much less likely to affect us negatively, because we're playing to our strengths. We're working with confidence in the arena in which we're the most comfortable and effective.

But the reality is that we all live with certain fears. We fear for the next medical report. We fear for a downturn in the economy. We fear for our children and their safety. Much of life is not within our control, and fear is simply a component of interacting with reality. We have to decide not to let fear be a primary driver.

MATERIALISM

Most of us are well-acquainted with the idea of materialism. It's one of the most influential drivers in our modern world, particularly in Western culture.

We want more. We want finer. We want better, once we see what the neighbors have.

We've established monetary wealth as the scoreboard by which we determine the winners and losers. Many of us will say, "Me, personally, I'm not money-driven." But we're not immune to the influences around us. This book's view of success has nothing to do with material things or money. But I'll be honest—I feel the same pull as everyone else. It's the world we inhabit.

We know what the scoreboard is, and it's human nature to want to outscore everyone else. Besides, who isn't attracted to the idea of limitless comfort and luxury? They have a price tag. The power to go where we want and to do what we want, to be free from the daily obligations of working and earning. Money is power, and that's another part of the attraction.

The undertow of materialism pulls at us every day, whispering that happiness and contentment are found through possessions, appearances, appetites, and all things shiny and tangible. Deep down, we know it's a lie. We realize inner qualities—integrity, faith, character—are much more important. But those qualities are invisible. You can't buy them. A new Tesla, however, is as tangible as it gets. An oceanfront property is irresistible.

We could have learned a lesson. American wealth plummeted 40 percent between 2007 and 2010. Just like that, all that money was vaporized. *Poof!* Was there ever a more vivid illustration of how fleeting monetary wealth is? Yet more than a decade has passed, and is anything different? Materialism has as sure a hold as ever.

The deception of that pursuit, of course, is that it's a journey with no arrival point. How much, exactly, is enough? Many people, having attained great success and wealth, look back and realize their happiest times actually came when they had very little—a starter home, an entry-level job, and the joy of relationships and plans for the future. Money is a means, something to exchange for something else, but at some point it *becomes* the something else for us. We want the money itself, and then we want more.

Think of the billionaires among us right now. None have announced, "I've earned all I want," though they'll never be able to spend even a portion of what they've accumulated. They compete with other billionaires. If only they could become trillionaires—maybe then they'd be content? I doubt it.

There was an interesting 2010 study, led by Nobel Prize–winning economists, about the actual price of happiness. It came to the conclusion that a $75,000 salary gets about as close as we can determine. From utter poverty up to that sum, "happiness" seems to grow; after $75,000, it stalls out. In other words, $150,000 doesn't make you twice as happy as 75. It may not make you happier at all. We should add that this was a North American study, geared to our standard of living.

The pursuit of money is a quest without a treasure, a rainbow with no pot of gold. And it's another driver that exhausts the soul.

CONSTANT NEED FOR APPROVAL

Are you a people pleaser? If so, what's wrong with that? There's not much point in displeasing people.

If you were the kid whose parents never came to your ball game or school program, or if you had to compete with other siblings for Mom's or Dad's time, you might have gotten into the flow of becoming a people pleaser. There are other reasons, of course. Many people are driven by the pursuit of approval. They're controlled by the expectations of others, or at least the desire to impress others.

People pleasers are very easy to manipulate because they have trouble saying no. Someone might think less of them, right? So certain folks pick up on these signals and take advantage of those with a constant need for approval. And, of course, after a while, when we feel used, we begin to feel anger and resentment—more unhealthy drivers.

It can work in different directions. I would love for my kids to think of me as the most generous, giving, and fun dad in the world. I love pleasing them. So it would be very easy for them to use my obvious delight and manipulate it. I would end up being driven in an unhealthy way, and they would end up spoiled and with unrealistic ideas of how the world works.

When we become obsessed with our standing with others, what we lose is our sense of ourselves. We neglect our own needs. We tend to be tired and frustrated, and do we ever really feel that we've earned the approval we crave? Even if we do, it seems we could lose it again.

What do all these drivers have in common? They all take control of someone's life, and they're all unhealthy. Now, it's true that some of these are harmless or even helpful in smaller doses. All of us want to please people; what would the world be like if no one cared what anyone else thought? It's a frightening idea.

But once the opinions of others overrule all other considerations, bad things happen in life. We go where others want us to go, instead of where we feel we should. We act in ways we think others will approve of, instead of in ways that are in tune with who we are at the core. No wonder a Google search on how to find happiness turns up six billion results!

THE STRESS BUCKET

There's an X factor among these drivers that also needs our attention. Whereas all of us fall prey to different drivers at different times, we all have to deal with a stress bucket. That's how I think of the ongoing level of anxiety we all carry. As I conceptualize it, each of us has a stress bucket. But stress doesn't evaporate on its own. The level builds up over time until it overflows.

Life is stressful, and when things aren't going right, the stress will catch up with us at some point, sometimes in puzzling ways that seem all out of proportion to what's going on.

I've recounted the occasion when I was driving my son to hockey practice, and a relatively small thing—a tip-off that a speed trap was ahead—caused me to melt down entirely. It was impossible to explain how such an utter, immobilizing panic attack could result from such a small thing. It just happened to be the one item that caused my stress bucket to overflow.

Managing stress is the topic for a whole other book. But it can also be handled through taking up a guided life instead of a driven one. As we care for ourselves in smarter ways, as we'll show in later chapters, that stress bucket never gets too full.

Better stress maintenance is just another angle to consider as we think about the strain of being driven instead of guided.

WHAT DRIVES YOU?

In our workshops, as I finish describing these six drivers, I ask, "Which of these drivers are influencing you right now?"

I can see the wheels turning. Brows are knit. Chins are stroked. I have yet to hear anyone claim they don't identify with any of these drivers. They tend to recognize several that are significant, but one or two that are primary. There's always a "chief suspect," a particular driver that clearly deserves their focus.

I ask those in the room to circle that driver in their notes, and perhaps to rate some of the others in their relevance. Someone might tell me, "Need for approval—that's me." Someone else will say, "I can't handle my anger. I've tried, and I just can't overcome it." How about you?

Know thyself is the starting point of personal growth. We identify the issue, and then—what are we going to do with it? Identifying the problem is essential, not just because you know where you stand, but because the knowledge of it motivates you to do something about it.

We place these drivers in the "past" category of our timeline, because that's where we'd like to keep them—firmly in the rearview mirror. But integrity compels us to be honest with ourselves about where we are in this moment. You may have strong, negative drivers in your life. This is a good time, as we finish this chapter, to take a careful look at your thoughts and emotions, and to come to some conclusions about what is driving you. But don't be discouraged if you don't like what you find. Identifying the drivers is the beginning of overcoming them. And there are practical steps you can take to be free of them.

If you struggle with guilt, knowing it and declaring it are empowering in themselves. You realize, "If I continue letting guilt call the shots in my life, I will never have any real happiness. I will never get where I want to go. I'll miss opportunities, I'll feel deeper anxiety, and I'll damage my relationships." Try squarely facing those realities every day for a week, and see if you're not energized to transform.

Second, if irrational emotions are controlling your life, you have to take back the controls. That means deciding where you want to go and how you're going to get there. And I believe the best way to do that is a life guided by purpose—the purpose you feel is the reason you're on this planet. In the next chapter, we're going to talk about that. We'll examine what it means to take control, and how you can begin to find your own purpose in life. I hope you're ready for a brand-new way of seeing your life.

In the meantime, it's helpful to think about that backpack you carry with you on your life journey. Space inside is at a premium. You don't want these negative drivers to spoil the elements of your life that go with you. If you take jealousy with you, or fear or resentment, it might be like a few bites of leftover egg salad sandwich, from last week's lunch, got into your pack. The smell would saturate, and pretty much ruin, everything you carried.

The drivers we've examined will do the same thing. They'll soak deeply into our talents, our gifts, our dreams, and everything that makes us who we are and guides us where we want to go.

Let's leave those behind us, move into a more promising present, and travel light.*

---

* For this section, in which we discuss emotional motivators in lives that aren't attuned toward purpose, I'm indebted to Rick Warren's wonderful book, *The Purpose Driven Life: What on Earth Am I Here For?* Those familiar with that book will recognize some similarities in concepts, though I move in a different direction with our Six Essentials in this volume.

CHAPTER THREE

FINDING YOUR WHAT AND WHY

"The only person you are destined to become is the person you decide to be."

—RALPH WALDO EMERSON

Sometimes you just need a job, period.

As a matter of fact, you more than likely started your work life right there: looking for a consistent paycheck. You were young, fresh from school, and your résumé was little more than a hopeful sheet of paper. Your plan was to make up for in energy what you lacked in expertise.

Unfortunately, all the CEO positions for Fortune 500 companies were filled at the moment. So it wasn't a matter of landing your dream job, whatever that was, or of finding the perfect fit. You needed to work, and that's how you entered the vast, complicated, contemporary marketplace.

But maybe you were fortunate enough to have a connection somewhere. Your family had a small business. Your buddy knew about an opening. Simple networking paid off. Or maybe you just pounded the pavement until you found something. Even then, you couldn't afford to be too choosy. If you were a square peg, you were willing to press yourself into a round shape, just to fit into the job opening, as long as it offered a dependable paycheck.

For months and then years, you simply went with the flow. You worked a job until a better one came along. There was always an implicit, if not explicit, understanding: *you* needed to be what the *job* required. The work was never going to readjust itself just to fit you, so if you worked for Acme Amalgamated Flux Capacitors, Inc., the passion of your life had to be flux capacitors (I dare you to google them). Advancement in the company depended upon selling these flux capacitors—and so did your grocery budget—so you needed to be all about them. You had to know everything about the kind you sold as well as the kind your competitors sold.

You did well. As time passed, networking and other considerations might have led to other industries and better opportunities. The guiding principle, however, was probably salary. That goes without saying. We all want to make a little more money, create a little more financial security, and provide a little more comfort to our families. And more money creates more freedom. So your career path took this turn and that twist, all based on finding better work and then adapting your interests to it.

In my own path, there was a point when I found myself involved with some university researchers in the University of Alberta. The scientists had created a new way to produce a radioactive isotope that could be used in cancer diagnosis, and to simplify a complex story, the world was looking for a new technology just like that.

I was in the right place at the right time.

I started a company with the researchers who invented this novel technology. As it turned out, we weren't able to move quite fast enough to make our product commercially viable. But sometimes I thought about my work with amusement: as a student, I'd hated the subjects of physics and chemistry. I was no scientist. And while I loved the idea of fighting cancer and saving lives, my motivation was market-based. This wasn't a passion for science; it was the best financial opportunity. It was a portfolio-builder.

It could have happened to you; perhaps something similar already has. It's actually a classic entrepreneurial story. Find what people are looking for, provide it, and there's money to be made—nothing wrong with that.

But there are other considerations that make the difference in how effective and how happy we are while we're making that money. Sometimes I had the thought, "How much more fun would this be if I were truly excited by the field of work?" I enjoyed it, but not in a way that was truly fulfilling.

Being productive is the great work we do with the best hours of our days. It makes a difference what work we choose. I've found that once we become square pegs trying to fit ourselves into round holes, a lot of us end up bent out of shape. The right fit is the one for which we feel a natural passion, and for which we're naturally equipped. That's when we excel.

I believe there's a you-shaped hole for everyone. To find that life purpose means to be forever guided by its pursuit, so that we're never driven by the emotions described in the previous chapter. We're guided by our purpose.

This chapter begins the process of finding that you-shaped hole in the world: the purpose you were born to uncover and follow. But what's the alternative?

LIFE WITHOUT PURPOSE

Have you ever seen the movie *Office Space*? It's a 1999 comedy as well as a ninety-minute study of what life is like when people are emotionally disconnected from their work. No wonder the movie was a hit with so many young adults who were then entering the workforce.

Peter Gibbons, the lead character, works in an office that is a mishmash of all the things we hate most about corporate North America. His workplace, Initech, is a vast, lifeless maze of cubicles. He has a boss, Lumbergh, who has zero personality, zero warmth, and a tendency of stopping by either to drone on about TP reports and their cover sheets, or to tell Peter, "Um, I'm gonna need you to come in on Saturday."

At one point Peter tells his hypnotherapist, "I was sitting in my cubicle today, and I realized, ever since I started working, every single day of my life has been worse than the day before it. So that means that every single day that you see me, that's on the worst day of my life."

"Is today the worst day of your life?" his hypnotherapist asks incredulously.

"Yes," says Peter.

"That's messed up, man."

Yes, it's messed up. The movie's one example of a happy individual is a character who is seriously injured in an automobile accident—the cash settlement enables him to patent a "jump to conclusions" mat, for literal jumping to various conclusions. It may not be the most marketable idea ever, but at least it lights him up inside. He's finally living the dream.

Office Space is the nightmare of everything we don't want our lives to become. Yet we all know people who have lost their sense of themselves in the cubicle-maze of the career journey. People today, at least as I observe them, are demanding the opportunity for a goal larger than Friday's paycheck. We're told that millennials and Gen Z, far more than previous generations, are proactively seeking out careers that offer a sense of something bigger than themselves. They won't willingly exchange their life and their time for a purpose that lacks passion for them. And if they have to spend a few years bussing tables in a restaurant or delivering pizzas, that's okay, if somewhere down the road it will help them move toward a life of greater meaning.

The children of the *Office Space* era are now coming of age. Many of them emerge from broken homes, as I did. Quite often, they've watched their parents grow older while serving out their time in careers they might even despise, given enough time.

And here we are: by 2025, three quarters of the global workforce will be composed of millennials. In a recent study, it was shown that seventy-five percent of millennials would be okay with a pay cut if it allowed them to work for a socially responsible company. That's a striking change from the career world we've observed in the past. These younger workers want to decide for themselves what constitutes a life of value and pursue it with monetary reward as a secondary objective.

More than ever, we are wondering about our What and our Why. It's not enough just to increase the net total of flux capacitors the company is churning out this fiscal quarter. We want to know how the flux capacitor contributes to the betterment of the world. Significance is a higher priority. *Why* are we doing what we're doing?

But the *What* comes into play, too, because it's not just about the significance of the product; it's also about who *we* are. Our work needs to be an expression of our personhood, our individuality. We're not interchangeable as people. We're not cogs in some machine. We know we have something to contribute that is wholly our own, and we want to make that connection through our work.

So we can define the quest for purpose as uncovering the work we're *uniquely designed* to do, and that work leads to something we care deeply about that makes a difference in the world.

BEGINNING THE QUEST

As I've described, I'm working with many people in this area of purpose. Most of these people are no longer in their twenties; they've had time to work in a company or two. They've notched a few successes. Many of them tend to be entrepreneurs, and so they're motivated people, goal-setters, and they're also people who think and reflect.

Many of them tell me they can't really identify a life purpose. They enjoy their work, but something is missing, somehow. Early on, at the beginning of adulthood, the great goal is to prove our capabilities—to show what we're made of. We do that. We score some points. We have some victories. But then comes a sense of "what else is there?"

I talk with these people about the What and the Why, and they're intrigued. Who could disagree about wanting to nail down those two questions? But they want to know...How?

My focus has shifted toward creating that How for these seekers of significance. To answer the question of What, I've developed the Temperature Check™. It's a kind of personal inventory, helping us find in ourselves the raw material necessary for discovering our purpose. The Check directs us to ask the right questions of ourselves, think carefully and honestly about our answers, and then discern the implications for our purpose in life. *What* do these questions indicate we should be doing?

The Temperature Check comes from the acronym TEMPS: *talents, experience, motivators, personality,* and *strengths.* These are five keys that tend to point to our What. They really begin the process of getting us moving in the right direction.

Then, having explored five questions for What, I offer what I call Getting to Why. Together, these are validators for who we are, what makes us unique, how we should use our gifts and values, and why they matter to us. These exercises are all about making sure we know who we are.

By this time, of course, many of us have taken various personality inventories and tests. Compared to times past, our generation has a strong self-analytical vocabulary. It's not unusual to hear even high achievers talk about having "a touch of ADHD," or to say, "I'm a type A personality," or something as simple as, "I'm a bit of a control freak." "I'm a people person" is a common self-evaluation. A century ago, people were less likely to think in these terms. In the age of psychology, we're much more interested in what makes each of us tick.

If you and I were talking, you could probably give me some basic personality information about yourself. And we'll say more about that topic of personality later. But the Temperature Check as a whole challenges us to think more about how we actually live, what kinds of activities we like or dislike, what gets us going, and what turns us off. I've found it to be very effective in opening new doors for people to understand who they are in terms of their best life.

Best of all, I see this as a simple and fairly painless test to help us get on the right path to a more fruitful and satisfying future. As I worked through these exercises myself, I was ultimately able to come up with a headline, a simplified mission statement, for who I am: *My purpose is helping others achieve success on purpose.* If my life has a bumper sticker, that's what's written on it. This book, my workshops, and everything I do flows naturally from my sense of purpose. This is the kind of focus I seek for all of us.

Therefore, all that we'll do in the balance of this book can be summarized by this outline:

1. Finding your purpose—your What and your Why. (Purpose)
2. Paring your activities down to the essentials of your purpose. (Focus)

3. Mastery in the course of the journey, through those essentials. (Flow)

That's the comprehensive scope of what we'll be doing. But it all begins with the first item, contained in the Temperature Check. It's going to help us make that transition from *driven* by every wind of change to *guided* toward a destination that feels custom-built for everything we are.

In the next chapter, we'll investigate the mystery of your destiny by looking for clues in five of the most important areas of your life. Be ready to examine them carefully. Sometimes they're elusive. I recommend having paper and pen nearby, or saving a voice memo on your phone—whatever works for you.

I also wouldn't recommend reading through the chapter in one quick sitting. Give it some time; your life and future are worth it. For each of the areas, consider taking a day to reflect deeply. Let the questions play around in the back of your mind during the day. You want the best, most thoughtful answers to questions like these.

Ready? Let's begin to explore the What and the Why that might define the rest of your life.

CHAPTER FOUR

THE TEMPERATURE CHECK

"When we strive to become better than we are, everything around us becomes better too."

—PAOLO COELHO

And so we come to this, your present moment in time—a time to take inventory of who you are and where you want to go. Here's your opportunity to take a good, long look in the mirror, examine your life, and decide how you see yourself at this moment of life. We'll examine five factors that point to the What for who you are.

We identify the Temperature Check as pertaining to the present, just as the drivers are (hopefully) relegated to the past. The TC is a way of taking a snapshot of who you are at this moment in time, though it also takes a look back at some of the influences that have molded you. It's important to visualize ourselves as standing at this present moment, recognizing the drivers we want to leave in the past, and using what we can identify in the backpack to make a wise course correction.

So, as you come to firm realizations about yourself in each of these categories, imagine placing them in your backpack. Consciously taking these identifiers with you is a matter of being true to yourself, and that will guide you toward happiness and success.

1. TALENTS

Let's start with your talents. These are skills, outstanding aptitudes you have in specific areas. What are you *great* at?

I'm talking about something you've naturally done with excellence for as long as you can remember. Not necessarily make-you-famous things such as singing, sports, or art. There are all kinds of talents.

I know some who have installed basketball hoops in their back-yard and shot thousands of free throws until they could hit a large number of them. That may reflect a desire to be good at shooting, but it's not a talent. Some people simply have specific skills built into their DNA. That was talent, and others could see it from the get-go.

One of my talents is public speaking. When I was in the fourth grade, our teacher staged a class debate (funny, the things we remember). The subject had to do with preserving land or developing it. It's not as if this was a topic I spent much time thinking about as a young boy. But when we got into the debate, I found I could speak well in front of the class. It just came naturally, working without notes and thinking on my feet in an engaging way.

There was a certain "buzz" I experienced in the feeling of holding a group's attention. No one trained me to do this; I never even saw it coming, to be honest. It was just there, part of who I was even at an early age.

I often read that fear of public speaking tops the list of things that frighten people the most. Fear of heights also makes the list; spiders and snakes tend to pop up. Some actually include zombies! But people are more frightened of public speaking? They'd rather take on a boa constrictor than talk to the Rotary Club? I don't get it, because it's something I was born to do. There are probably other things I can't imagine taking on, however, that you naturally master. Talents are distributed among us in unpredictable ways.

So where are you truly talented? What is the area where you were born to excellence? As you think about that, factor in the extent to which it gives you joy. Lots of people take piano or guitar lessons. Some are born with the musical gift, and it shows up in the way they can't go through a day without expressing their love of music in some way. There has to be a piano or a guitar nearby or life isn't right.

I've heard people say, "Oh, I don't have any talents." I believe they haven't thought it through enough; everyone has certain areas where they naturally excel. Talents and gifts don't have to be dramatic. Public speaking certainly isn't. The ability to mentally organize large numbers of details isn't. The ability to connect with people in such a way that you can lead them isn't. Yet these abilities can be very valuable if used in the right places.

I'm not going to offer you a comprehensive list of every talent on earth. No one could do that. But I'm going to direct you to think long and hard about what you do well and truly enjoy doing. Put the book down right now and begin to write down your list of talents. While you're thinking and writing, notice your emotions and how you feel when you're exercising your talents. If you have trouble evaluating yourself, check the list of talents that follows as you decide what goes in the backpack.

SAMPLE LIST OF TALENTS

ARTISTIC	Playing an instrument. Woodworking. Graphic design.
ATHLETIC	Balance. Coordination. Rhythm.
ACADEMIC	Strategic thinking. Mathematical thinking. Problem-solving.
COMMUNICATION	Storytelling. Writing. Brainstorming.
INTERPERSONAL	Caring for others. Listening. Leadership.
RELATIONAL	Intuitive. Organized. Staying calm under pressure.

2. EXPERIENCES

The next part of this Temperature Check involves thinking back over your life. What are the experiences that formed you?

This is really about figuring out how you've been shaped and molded by life. There were certain life lessons that profoundly impacted your development. I was an only child. I had to find friends and build those same-age relationships I needed. To this day, I make friends easily, and I trace that all the way back to my childhood. I was also formed by some tough experiences and brokenness in my family, and these things have molded the way I look at being a husband and a father.

In college, I had a hockey coach who was tough and demanding—just a hard-ass in every way. Once, I was hit in the side of the head by a water bottle he'd kicked across the bench in a fit of anger in the middle of a game. Our team was strong; we went undefeated that year and won the national championship. But our coach never let up, never showed a softer side when dealing with his players. If we were winning by two goals and it should have been four, he gave us hell over it.

He eventually made it to the NHL as an assistant coach. He was good at what he did. Years after he coached me, I called him up and thanked him—*not* for screaming or raging, but for pushing me toward being my best, going all out, and never settling for anything but the top of my potential. At the time, I didn't see him as a mentor, but I learned valuable things from him. I don't have to take the part about rarely affirming his players, but I can certainly use his insistence on excellence. In fact, I look at all my work through that lens today.

Later, coming out of college, I took a job selling home security systems on 100 percent commission. I had to live completely on sales with no salary—and I was terrible at it. I never made a single sale, nor did I enjoy a single second of my work. From that experience, I learned what kind of sales I *didn't* want to do.

Then I worked for a credit agency, and it was my job to convince people to keep up with their car payments. I watched my coworkers make phone calls to the nonpayers and begin screaming at them and berating them. What I learned was, off the ice, you could catch more flies with honey than with vinegar. So while I didn't stay in that profession, I took a good lesson away from it about how to communicate hard things to people and compel them to act in a productive manner.

So what we're looking for here is what you've experienced, how you've reacted, and what you've learned about yourself. And it's less about generalized lessons (such as catching flies with honey) than what it revealed about me (my personality being much more geared to positive, relational approaches). If you think about a formative experience in your life and something about it had a tremendous impact on you, there's a reason for that impact. Somebody else might not even have noticed, but you responded in such a way that it stands out in your memory. What does it say about you and how you're wired?

In schools, what courses did you hate and which ones caught your interest? Were you drawn to math, science, or English? What kinds of friends did you enjoy spending your time with, and which ones irritated you?

As you can imagine, this is a provocative exercise. There's a lot to think about, and it might be the first time you've reviewed these memories in such a light. What's your experiential education?

Put the book down right now and begin to write down your list of experiences. While you're thinking and writing, notice your emotions and how you feel about what's coming to mind for you. Think specifically in the following areas of your life:

⇒ **Family.** What were the great lessons of life that came from your home life and upbringing?
⇒ **Educational.** In school, which subjects did you enjoy, achieving your best results?

- **Vocational.** In what career occasions were you the happiest and most effective? Why?
- **Spiritual.** Thinking about the universe or God, when have you been the most spiritually inclined and what influence did it have on you?
- **Painful.** Think of the more difficult trials of your life. What lessons did you bring away from them? Where do you find resiliency from the inevitable 'downs' of life?

3. MOTIVATORS

Now we're thinking about *fuel*, and this one's more about right now. What gets you excited?

These are matters you find yourself caring about. Again, they will be tied to experiences and what you remember of them, but the important element this time is care and connection.

I'm highly motivated to be the best father I can be. This is tied to my experience as a child and my feelings about experiencing a broken home. I also remember experiencing life in a large, comfortable house with a swimming pool, then losing all that when my father's business failed. These were the early years of my life, the most impressionable years, and I emerged with strong feelings about what makes a good father.

Charles Darwin ultimately helped us develop the theory of evolution, but he wasn't thought to be very intelligent as a boy. He collected dead things. He spent hours lifting rocks and peering under them. He was intrigued by the tiny ecosystems he found there, the kinds of insects that thrived. He took long walks through the woods just to observe. Nature was his first love, his motivating factor, and that moved him toward his life work.

Money is a motivation for me, as it is for many of us, but it's far from the only one. I care about earning a comfortable income, but because I have deep emotions about what life was like for me before I uncovered my purpose, I care even more about helping other people uncover theirs. It's simply what I feel compelled to do.

Our motivations come from deep desires, and this is why we have to do some deep thinking to bring these desires to the surface. What do you care deeply about?

I've known people who have found themselves gravitating in certain career directions they didn't originally intend.

Let's say Jennifer is an accountant, and she likes her job. It pays the rent; she gets along with coworkers. One day, her company begins to support the cause of helping the local downtown food bank. Jennifer and her friends help sort canned foods. As she leaves, she feels really good about her efforts. It was kind of fun, kind of meaningful. Later, she finds herself returning, on her own, to help out—but in the mission's office. Something clicks for her; she loves this work, knowing it feeds people. Now she helps run food banks in a network of cities.

Again, it's about who we already are, how we're made, and how we can get more in tune with our basic nature. So what motivates you? When you're surfing the web, what kinds of subjects galvanize you? What discussions are you attracted to on Facebook? How and where do you volunteer your time, and what subjects do you enjoy learning about? Give some thought to the relevant hot buttons in your life.

Put the book down right now and begin to write down your list of what motivates you. While you are thinking and writing, notice your emotions and how you feel about what is coming to mind for you.

SAMPLE LIST OF MOTIVATORS

HELPING	Environmental. Social. Governance.
WINNING	Competition. Achievement. Earning.
POWER	Recognition. Influence. Directing.
GROWTH	Change. Improvement. Innovation. Curiosity.

4. PERSONALITY

In the previous chapter, we mentioned this key consideration. Up to now, the Temperature Check has called on you to evaluate yourself. These calls have been a matter of judgment. It's a good idea to ask others to help you look at yourself objectively; they'll offer observations that might surprise you. But still, it's been mostly about how you understand yourself. Only you know what motivates you, the impact of your experiences, and what talents are closest to your heart.

Personality can be measured a bit more scientifically. Today we have an array of tests and assessments that can help us learn a lot about who we are. In all likelihood, you probably have experience with some of these tests. It's common now for companies and placement agencies to use them. Some are online; some, of course, are more helpful than others.

On the most basic level, most people have some idea whether they're introverts, extroverts, or some blend of the two. As an introvert, you're more reserved, more reflective, and perhaps most comfortable working alone. As an extrovert, you're highly social and gain energy when around people.

It's not a binary distinction, of course, nor are we each located on a scale between the two. We're all a bit more complex than that. For example, you might feel introverted in certain matters and more extroverted in others. I know I'm an extrovert, and I enjoy being with people. But I also find solitude rewarding and reenergizing at times.

This is where assessments come in; they can help us better understand how we function in different kinds of settings.

IQ tests may be the most recognizable assessment. We think of these tests as simple measurements of basic intelligence. But human intelligence is too complex to be measured by a simple test. For example, there's EQ, which is emotional intelligence and is indicated on a whole different scale. Obviously you could have a high IQ and an abysmal EQ—or vice versa. Some even believe that IQ and EQ are inversely proportional. The stereotype would be the "nerd" with no social skills—such as the character of Sheldon on *The Big Bang Theory*—and the loving nurturer who isn't very sophisticated but always has a hug handy.

What's higher for you: IQ or EQ? Are you better at solving equations or comforting sad people? EQ measures our ability to identify, evaluate, control, and express emotions. Since relationships are based on the finer points of understanding and communicating with each other, those with higher EQ can become strong leaders, and they tend to function well in a team setting. What about the person with the higher IQ? This person has strong thinking and problem-solving skills, and may or may not be a team person. He or she will excel at thinking through the dynamics of a complicated issue.

The Myers-Briggs Type Indicator is one example of a more in-depth inventory than a binary test. It ultimately divides people into sixteen personality types. For every test, of course, there's a debate on its accuracy. And in the end, such tests measure how we see ourselves, which is always subjective. But in my experience, people who take at least one of these thorough tests feel they've received valuable insight into how they think and behave.

The Kolbe A Index is one I've found helpful. Using thirty-six questions, it focuses on our thinking by measuring our instincts—conative strengths. This is an alternative to emphasizing personality traits or learned skills, in an attempt to find out who we really are beneath all that. The approach is toward our natural behavior in specific situations.

The approach of the **Watson-Glaser Critical Thinking Appraisal**, on the other hand, is to gauge our ability to analyze and interpret written information, then draw logical conclusions. It actually uses a series of tests that help us understand how we understand communication and make decisions.

I strongly recommend that you take at least one or more thorough personality tests in order to come to a better understanding of how your personality is best understood. With a base understanding of your ability to empathize, reason, problem-solve, and take action, you are well on your way to a higher level of self-awareness.

Once you have collected the results from your chosen assessments, take some time to process what you've learned about yourself. Then return to this book study and incorporate your new understandings into your list, which so far includes your inventory of talents, experiences, and motivations.

5. STRENGTHS

Strengths? But...we've already discussed talents. What's the difference between strengths and talents?

Remember our guy who installs a basketball hoop in his backyard? Maybe he remembers playing as a kid, when he couldn't make a shot from one foot away. He shoots one hundred free throws every day, just after work and only for nostalgia, and becomes really good at it. Is this a talent? No, but it's become a strength—and that's something to be proud of. And while basketball isn't going to be a *marketable* strength for him, perseverance will be.

I tend to stress talents, personality, and those things that are part and parcel of who we are because they become the best indicators of what we should do. But it's also true there are people who have become incredibly competent without having had an ounce of talent or natural ability in that direction.

We all know the stories of professional athletes who were thought to be no more than marginally talented, yet became the best at their profession. Kurt Warner stocked grocery store shelves for $5.50 per hour. He'd played a little football for Northern Iowa, but he wasn't even close to being a draft choice.

Yet he ended up a Super Bowl MVP, a regular All-Pro, and an NFL

MVP twice. He had some talent, clearly, but his other character strengths had to elevate that talent. We're thankful life works this way, because being born with a world-class talent, or not, isn't the end of the story. Hard work keeps a lot of doors and windows open to us, even when we don't feel good enough.

Jim Collins preaches this concept in his popular book, *Good to Great: Why Some Companies Make the Leap...and Others Don't*. A lot of people, and a lot of companies, start with roughly the same raw materials. All of the businesses he analyzes are *good*. But the ones who become great make themselves so through rugged dedication.

What strengths are on your side? Gallup, the poll group, developed an online tool called CliftonStrengths (formerly StrengthsFinder). It's an assessment completely dedicated to personal strengths in strategic thinking, relationship-building, influencing, and executing, and I know a lot of people who have found it valuable. We all need a good, objective measurement of where we're at our best.

Put the book down right now and begin to write down your list of strengths, as you've come to understand them. What have you developed over the course of your life's journey so far?

SAMPLE LIST OF STRENGTHS

COMMUNICATION	Verbalize ideas clearly and concisely. Provide constructive criticism. Active listening.
LEADERSHIP AND MANAGEMENT	Clear expectation setting. Effective delegation to achieve desired result. Create a compelling vision.
DECISIVENESS	Best course of action. Implementation of plans. Follow-up and accountability.
PROBLEM-SOLVING	Understand cause-and-effect relationships. Ability to simplify. Identify root cause of issues.

What paths towards mastery are you on? While you're thinking and writing, notice your emotions and how you feel about what is coming to mind for you.

That's the Temperature Check to help you uncover your What. But having thought about those questions, there's another angle we need to take in learning what you're meant to do.

GETTING TO WHY

Not only do we seek our What, but we seek our Why. We're speaking now about the future, because this is about setting the intention of what we want our life to be. Sure, we want to know what we're seeking to accomplish, but we must know why that's so. It comes down to who we are and what we care deeply about. Once we can be firm about our What and our Why, we have a sense of purpose, and the future is wide open to us.

If you've worked through the previous pages carefully, you should have quite a few notes about who you are based on your talents, experiences, motivators, personality, and strengths. You might have twenty items, or you might have fifty. So how do you assemble this data? Taken together, what does the sum of it indicate about you?

Have you ever asked yourself the question, what do you really want your life to be about? As some would put it, what is the True North of your inner being? The following five questions are designed to help you uncover the answer. Once again, take some time with each of these factors. They probe the mystery of the essential you—the intentional you.

1. CORE VALUES

Core values determine who we really are, at the core of our personhood. And what determines that? It's the compilation of our experiences in life, our biology and genetics, of the items we explored in the Temperature Check—these are the most important beliefs that have created a core set of timeless principles that we hold dear; the nonnegotiables that we don't just give lip service to, but would defend passionately.

For that reason, our core values set the target for what kind of person we'd like to be. They may be the things you'd like to have said about you at your funeral, when those you love rise to offer a eulogy. Have you already thought of some of these?

Try to make a list of three to seven prominent values you expect to persevere and to strengthen as you move forward. Think of words such as trustworthy, compassionate, leadership, courageous, and loyal.

Make your own list; don't model it on anyone else's or take it from a company website. But here is a typical list:

→ A belief in family as an essential of life.
→ A belief in being a good steward of resources and in exercising humility.
→ A belief in all-embracing integrity and trustworthiness.
→ A belief in a healthy balance between life, work, and recreation.
→ A belief in God/spirit/universe.
→ A belief in creative solutions to important problems.
→ A commitment to serving people and my community.

Your list doesn't even need to sound like that one. Your list could be individual words, or a couple of sentences. There isn't a right or wrong way, other than the need for it to represent your core.

Here's another helpful exercise. Write down the names of three people you personally know well, and about whom you think the following: if everyone in your life was like these three people, you could accomplish nearly anything. You'd be surrounded by excellence.

Then, with those three names written down, list the characteristics you admire about them. What is it that draws you to them so strongly?

From your list, select three to seven core values that stand out. Here are examples from my own list: *purpose guided, do the right thing, help first, humbly confident,* and *thirst for learning.* When you've assembled your own list, you should be looking at a collection of *core values.*

It's become a popular term. Not just individuals, but businesses are identifying several core values that are basic to who they are as a company and that never change. You might find several core values for your life, but if you list twenty, you've gone beyond the essential. Try to get to the very center of your identity. Less is more.

No one possesses the perfect "value set," and most of us major on certain attributes. We have our points of strength. Perhaps "thirst for learning" doesn't resonate with you, for example, but loyalty strikes a chord. Perhaps trustworthiness is a hallmark that others have pointed out about you, and you were surprised, because you simply took it for granted. Remember, we're talking about something you see in yourself that you want to take into the future with you—something that will be at the center of what you do. Spend some time thinking about your core values now *and* the person you seek to become.

2. PRIORITIES

The next consideration is this: what will you prioritize? When all the trappings are removed, all the activities, the pieces of identity, and the things life simply requires of you (as opposed to what you'd rather do)—where will you spend your time, energy, and resources? Who are you when no one else is around and life makes no particular requirements of you?

Sometimes I hear, "What I really care about is family. My family is everything for me, and I'll do whatever it is in life that helps me strengthen and care for my spouse, my children, my home."

Someone else might say, "I want to make a great name for myself. When I die, I want my obituary to speak of some achievement that will give me a place in history long after I'm gone. I want to make a genuine impact." Or another person might say, "I want to leave the world a better place than I found it. I want to do something that improves society in some way."

Sometimes people realize an activity they've viewed as merely a hobby is actually their innermost essential passion. That's their sweet spot—their focus.

Others admit they want to enjoy life—no more, no less than that. They figure they'll go around once in this life, and they want to have fun while they do.

Some are inspired by altruism or politics or some other guiding light. Others want to accumulate wealth. If so, by the way, fine—there's no judgment in this exercise. This isn't about what we think we *should* do; it's an honest realization of what we want to do. So as you think about your priorities, be honest above all.

3. LEGACY

Visualize your funeral after a long and productive life. What would you like to hear in the eulogy? How would you like to be remembered? Legacy is all about what we've done to make the world a better place. It's possible there are people who see their true purpose as becoming the richest person in the world, or to live to climb the seven highest peaks on each continent.

But even in such cases, the people I've come across, the people who would read this book, have been caring people. They've been people who want to give back. In other words, they want to create a legacy. Maybe it's to decrease world hunger or poverty. Maybe there's a spiritual or religious component. Perhaps it's to create beauty through architecture or some other art form, or to bridge political gaps between people. Generally, there's a contribution to society they want to make.

I see my legacy as the people I've directly helped to guide toward their life purpose. That could be through seminars, speaking engagements, personal relationships, or some other form of interaction. As I go about each new week of work, this is something I think about. How many people have I really transformed? What percentage of those people will have gained some advantage in turning their lives toward the adventure of a committed purpose? The idea of a future legacy motivates me every day.

As you think through this idea, I challenge you to be specific and personal. It's not particularly helpful to say, "My legacy is to have been a good husband and father," or "to be remembered as a kind and helpful human being." These ideas are far too general. What problem in the world would you like to fix? What kinds of people would you like to help? And then, how are you specially equipped through your gifts, talents, and your core values to do that? Remember, in life purposes, everything comes together. You wouldn't have a legacy that didn't spring from your core values or that you lacked the talent to pursue.

A century from now, what will people say about you? If they look you up on that generation's version of Wikipedia, what will they find?

4. COMMUNITY

There's also a social factor. Our big ideas and our core values inevitably point to the world around us and the people we care about. As I've said, the kind of people who would read this book are not lone rangers. They're not the type who stay to themselves. They're social beings; they're caring people. I believe that's actually a normal attribute of the human race. Life doesn't work well outside of the idea of community.

So this fourth factor has to do with what we want to do for others. As we move forward toward our purpose, we find ourselves moving from *me* to *we*. Even as we work for our own good, most of us want others to benefit from our efforts as well. We're not independent agents in this world. We become more and more aware of our context. We want our work to reverberate through the people and the world around us.

There's another element to the idea of community. We also aspire to enjoy a certain level of relationships with the kind of people we admire. I can speak for my own aspirations: I want to be around the community of positive people who want to continue to grow and learn and change. I can feel pleasure in finding and pursuing purpose in my life, but I can't feel true, full pleasure unless I see the same thing happening for people I care about. Obviously, those are people I work with, speak to, counsel with, write for. They're my community, and they're an essential part of my life purpose—which wouldn't even have a context or meaning without them.

Think about who "your people" are or would be, if you could spend your time with anyone you chose; if you could attend a convention for one type of person, soak up the wisdom there, and eventually become a member—what community would it be?

5. MESSAGE

Finally, there must be a communique—something you want your

community to know. That's your message. If you were to put one bumper sticker on your car, on any subject, what would it be? What's the message that's most important to you? What's ahead is your opportunity to *speak it into existence.*

If you saw a car turning the corner toward someone crossing the road, you'd have an urgent message, and you wouldn't be satisfied to hold it in your heart; you'd want it delivered immediately! Message: "Get off of the road!" We're not talking about personal and private reflections here, but that kind of message that makes you ache because everyone else doesn't yet feel about it the way you do.

You find yourself becoming an evangelist of that message, inserting it into conversations, speaking up in places you normally wouldn't be so assertive. And you speak this message without reservation, without concern about what others may think. You're as loyal and faithful to this message as you are to a close family member. And sometimes, you get the thrill of seeing people around you begin to pick up on that message and speak it themselves. It's out there now, and maybe it will continue to spread. And you realize few things are more important to you than that.

Do you have a message like that?

As I work with groups of people, I often see individuals struggle at this point. They're uncertain about a "message." They work. They strive. They haven't thought about having something to *say* about it. At this point, I'm not shy about asking them, "Do you know what your purpose in life is? Do you know why you're here and what you're supposed to be doing?" Of course, that's the whole objective of this book, but the idea of message is central to that. If you have a strong central purpose, you'll have something to say to your community about that. And if you happen to already have something to say to the world, a Big Idea that doesn't come or go, but stays close to your heart—that may be the single greatest clue to your purpose.

Another way of thinking about it is that your message is close to the legacy you've been thinking about. What is the idea you want to be associated with long after you're gone? If there's no one great idea or initiative to which you've hitched your soul, you'll have a hard time finding a true sense of purpose. So taking some real time to reflect on this one is well worth your while.

My message, as I've said, is delivered through workshops, talks, facilitation, and writing this book. I prioritize activities that give my message the best chance of being heard in the hopes of leaving a positive legacy. I have powerful core beliefs about the meaning of purpose in life, and I'm trying to speak them into existence through what I do. Do you have a message that you want to tell your community, or perhaps the entire world?

* * *

Congratulations! You've worked through the Temperature Check including the "Getting to Why" portion. You should now have a good bit of information about who you are, why you're that way, and who you want to become. Some of your realizations may even have come as a surprise to you.

I mentioned earlier that we're trying to solve a mystery. In a mystery novel, the detective embarks on an investigation, assembling all the clues and following their implications until they lead to a solution.

After completing these exercises, your initial investigation is complete. As you look at the results of these ten What and Why indicators, you should have an abundance of clues—telling suggestions about your life, your activities, your interests, your passions, and your aspirations for the future. We've examined how you see yourself now and how you dream about your future.

Lay it all out—are you developing a strong idea of what you're all about? A recurring theme that keeps finding its way into all the categories? Then take all that you've laid out (on screen, paper, or in your imagination) and make a list of those essential elements of who you are, who you care about, what you believe, what you prioritize, what you tell others about, what you're made to do, and what matters to you more than anything else. Study that list well, and place each item in that backpack you've visualized. They should be the things you can't imagine yourself leaving behind.

Of course, there's one more question you ask before a journey: Left anything behind? Anything missing from the list? Think hard. Take another day or two if you need it. The journey begins immediately, so be ready to travel.

CHAPTER FIVE

YOUR FOCUS AND FLOW

"Keep your face to the sunshine and you can never see the shadow."
—HELEN KELLER

Michelangelo was an outstanding Italian artist during the Renaissance—an elite painter, architect, and even a poet. But in his mind, the only art that counted was his sculpture. He was constantly under pressure to paint such masterpieces as the Sistine Chapel walls and ceiling. His talents in many arts were in high demand, but all he really wanted to do was carve out of stone.

Michelangelo had a philosophy of work. He would personally select the massive block of marble from its quarry. It had to be the most unblemished specimen of stone he could find. Then he'd begin his work, chipping away at that block with his chisel, dust flying as he worked.

Michelangelo explained his approach this way: "I saw the angel in the marble, and I carved until I set him free." That is, he meticulously removed everything in the stone that was *not* the angel. Thus a plain block of rock became an awesome work of art.

In 1501 Michelangelo began with the end in mind when creating his masterpiece, David. In 1989, Stephen Covey popularized that saying in *The 7 Habits of Highly Effective People*. The sculptor began with the end in mind—his vision—and one chunk of raw stone. Then he set about patiently, bit by bit, subtracting everything that was not part of that vision.

In the end, that's what all of us must do, if we are to realize our full potential. We have to carve away everything that isn't the "angel." We can't afford the clutter of extraneous items and dead-end tangents.

I know it's no easy task from my own experience. We're sidetracked by this uninvited distraction and that alluring opportunity. Something leaps into view that seems like a worthy cause at the time. We take a short detour from the main road; tomorrow, another one. We find there are distractions within distractions. Add up enough sharp turns, worthy as they may be in the short run, and we find we're moving in circles, filling our lives with causes and concerns that have nothing to do with carving out our life's masterpiece.

As you worked through the exercises in the previous chapter, you probably found yourself thinking a great deal about your time, your priorities, and what you'd like to see happen in the years ahead.

Your life is all about a key objective, and you're ready to go after it with all your heart, mind, and soul. This book is all about how to reduce what's weighing down your life and get down to what really counts.

Getting to that point is a function of time. It can't be completed in a weekend seminar or the course of reading a book—that's why we describe a journey rather than an experience. While you may already be getting a good idea of your purpose, it will evolve, solidify, and become more focused over time. It's important to realize we're talking about a lifelong process. But where do you go from here?

That's where the Six Essentials™ come in.

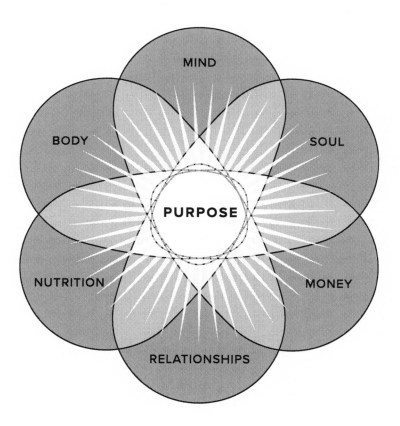

THE SIX ESSENTIALS

Purpose as a destination is a function of why you are on this earth and what you are here to accomplish in the time you're given—time, simply because of the complexity of life. It takes time to put a fine point on what that purpose is, and it also takes time to prune away everything that detracts from what's really important to you. Once you're sure what your life is all about, you'll realize you want to make the best possible use of time in getting there.

It's a function of why you're here because you'll never persevere at a task that doesn't speak to your soul and compel you at the deepest level. Knowing your why will help you break through times of discouragement. It will give you the willpower to avoid distractions and the pressure that comes from people who have different agendas for you.

In the last chapter, we focused a great deal on the ideas and activities you're passionate about, because it's not enough simply to decide what you *should* do with your life; you also must *yearn* to do it.

You may have heard the name Napoleon Hill. His 1937 book *Think and Grow Rich* is one of the most influential books of its kind in history. He said that successful giants of commerce shared two factors: they all had the strong belief they would succeed, and they had the kind of all-out desire and persistence we've just described.

We have an innate ability to manifest our dreams in the real world—to be the captains of our own destiny. That's a powerful concept. Have you noticed? If we begin to believe we're sick, it becomes so. People who expect to do well are far more likely to do well. There's so much power simply in what we believe about ourselves. Realizing this should cause us to stop and ask: What do I believe about myself? Am I self-confident? Do I see myself reaching my goals, or do I think negatively and create a self-fulfilling prophecy about myself?

To reach your desired destination, you'll need passion and confidence over time. That's the equation. But you'll need a little more than that. You'll need to do a little sculpting of your life, Michelangelo-style. The series of six essentials we're about to examine will provide powerful assistance. We'll describe six areas where you can chip away at everything keeping you from being successful.

These aren't items you need to go out and acquire; they're already ingredients of who you are. They're actually the very elements that make us human. But everything depends upon what we do with them, how we develop them, and how we nurture and improve them.

If we have this innate power to proactively shape our destiny, then it's entirely possible we can find our purpose, set our minds upon it, and travel the road of fulfilling it. So, in this chapter, you'll find the basic plan that can be used throughout your life; it's all here—which doesn't mean it's going to be easy. Life will still throw all the same obstacles at us. This is the navigation system, the vehicle for getting there, and you have to maintain it.

Think about physical travel. If you buy a car to take you across the country, you'll need to do more than put gas in it. You'll need to think about oil, various engine functions, the wear on the tires, the battery, and any number of other moving parts beneath the hood. These six essentials are like those. Maintain them and your journey will move smoothly and effectively.

And remember your backpack, even if you're taking the car for this analogy. As you think through these six key areas of your life, you'll be adding and subtracting things based on that all-important destination. We'll continue to talk about the backpack.

What are the Six Essentials™?

⇒ Mind
⇒ Body
⇒ Soul
⇒ Nutrition
⇒ Money
⇒ Relationships

Study that list, and you'll agree that each of these represents a piece of your identity. Yet each of us has a different combination of how we handle them. It's also true that they're interconnected. Body and nutrition are closely related. Mind and soul, too. For that matter, the mind touches on *all* of these, which is why we discuss it first.

In one or two of these areas, you might say, "I'm at my best here. In terms of my body, I go to the gym five times a week. I'm in the best physical fitness of my life." Fantastic. And if you're taking the right steps there, you might also be feeding your body intelligently, providing the right nutrition. So perhaps in those two areas, you're already ahead of the game.

But then your eye falls upon the word *soul*, and you might be a little more ambivalent. You might not even be too sure about the meaning of that one. Or relationships—how are you doing there? For each of us, there will be strong areas and more problematic ones.

The point is that *all six* are incredibly important. It's not a "pick any four of the following" type of exercise. And even in areas where you might feel you're excelling, there's always room to improve.

There's a lot to think about here, and for many of us, it will probably be the first time we've deeply reflected on all of these topics—not to mention all of them in their interrelationships with each other. It's also unlikely you've ever considered these as elements in fulfilling your life purpose.

Therefore, you are cordially invited to spend some time with each of these following six chapters. Learn a little more about each significant side of who you are; reflect on where you stand with each one, and learn some practical ways you can grow in each area.

If you continue to sharpen your mind, care for your body, deepen your soul, improve your nutrition, master your money, and strengthen your relationships, not only will you create the optimal conditions to manifest your purpose—you'll simply become an incredibly impressive human specimen! That's no shabby goal in itself.

For now, let's take a quick look at these six areas and establish what we mean by them.

MIND

Your mind is mission control for your life. All your thoughts, all your emotions, all your memories, and all your decisions originate in this one mysterious center that lies north of your neck and between your ears.

Do you control your thoughts, or do your thoughts control you? The answer is slipperier than you may think. The brain is a perpetual motion machine. It never stops, even while you're sleeping. Everything involves thought. If your spouse says, "Let's decide about dinner," you quickly guide your thoughts in that direction, pull some mental files, and cogitate on what you'd like to do for dinner. You're operating the controls in your mind.

But what about those moments when you're driving, or daydreaming, or sitting in a waiting room, and your thoughts seem to drift here and there on their own? We have thoughts we didn't initiate, some of them emotional, such as, *Why did that person say that thing that offended me?* It turns out your mind has a mind of its own!

In this next chapter, we're going to be thinking about thinking— something we do all too rarely. We'll focus not on deciphering the mysteries of thought, but on harnessing the direction of our thinking—taking control of our conscious thought so that our body's mission control center will work more toward the goal of life purpose, rather than random or disorganized thinking.

All six essential life factors begin with the mind.

BODY

If the mind is mission control, the body is the vessel that carries out its instructions. Our human anatomy may be a bit less mysterious than the mind, but it's just as complex. As a matter of fact, it's the most wonderful machine in the history of earth, and because we live within that machine, we often take it for granted.

In elementary schools, there's a teaching tool known as the Visible Man and the Visible Woman. This is a plastic model of the human body that generally sits on a table somewhere in the classroom. Its "skin" is clear plastic, so kids can see all the bodily organs that make up the human design. (You can see the twenty-first-century version of the Visible Human at www.bodyworlds.com, or the exhibitions that tour the country.)

At some point in time, children would look at that table model and think, "Is all of this inside of me?" If you opened the Visible Woman, you could see the digestive system, with its fifteen feet of intestines efficiently coiled. You could see the red-and-blue highway map known as the circulatory system, the muscles, the nerves, the respiratory system with its expanding and contracting lungs, and beneath it all, a sturdy skeleton. How could all of that fit in one body? How does the mind keep all those operations working with perfect efficiency?

This organic, flesh-and-blood machine is marvelous, but we're only allotted one per lifetime. There are no upgrades. It's designed to last for all the wear and tear of an ordinary life—if we care for it.

What if you were gifted a brand new Bugatti La Voiture Noire, the world's most expensive automobile at more than $18 million? Would you take special care with it, or neglect its engine, its perfect paint, and its lovely interior, and treat it like a lemon from the used car lot?

The body deserves reverent care. It has no price tag, because without it, you're not even here. When we get to this chapter, we'll look at some highly practical, even pleasant ways to maintain the machine that will determine just how successful and comfortable your life can be.

SOUL

Did we agree that the mind is mysterious? How about the soul? With some people, its very existence is in dispute. Is the human soul a *thing*? If so, where is it located? What exactly does it "do"? And does it continue to exist once bodily life comes to an end?

It's also a difficult topic for discussion because many of us have our own religious ideas of what the soul might—or might not—be. All the world's major religions deal with the soul and various stances on its definition and understanding. None of this constitutes the discussion we want to have, however. We're interested in the generally accepted idea that all of us have a kind of essence, a unique identity that transcends all the rest of our faculties. Many of us have the idea that the soul actually touches eternity—or at least some greater level of existence—rather than simply this bodily life.

So what does any of that have to do with defining our purpose? My opinion is that in today's very busy, very materially driven world, the soul is the easiest part of us to neglect. Yet if it's the expression of who we truly are, as opposed to all other people on this planet, we need to be in touch with the soul. We need to nurture it. That needn't be exclusively a religious expression. In this chapter, we'll look at practical ways we can care for the soul and become deeper and wiser people who approach our sense of purpose with a more informed, more nuanced understanding of who we really are.

This chapter will approach the topic much as twelve-step groups approach the spiritual side of things. "Anon" groups speak of a "higher power" without tying that concept down to any doctrinal direction. We should be able to discuss the human soul with an openness based on the concepts and experiences we all share as human passengers of this spinning planet.

NUTRITION

Nutrition? Haven't we already included the body as a topic? But this one's a little different. Here, we're talking about one of the primary considerations when it comes to caring for our physical health. Food deserves a chapter of its own.

From our earliest years of life, we're told to eat right. That message begins with our parents, then in school we're taught the idea of a balanced meal. It can all become caught up in guilt, evidenced by the way we speak of "comfort food" and use eating as some kind of emotional crutch. The roads are packed with fast food chains that dress up their wares in bright colors and imagery designed to make the mouth water. The fact is that so many of the things we're told not to eat are the very things that taste the best!

Yet all the while, we know that food is fuel. Again, if you owned the world's finest automobile, would you fill it with cheap gas?

Leaving the idea of purpose completely aside, we can agree that at the very least, we want to live longer and be healthier. We certainly don't want heart disease or the problems that come with obesity. So the reasons for good nutrition are baked in, so to speak.

But even more, as we begin to view ourselves as people on a mission, people out to achieve something exciting and important to us, we want all the time and all the health available to us. If we can be active and fruitful at seventy or eighty, we want that opportunity. And we're so much more likely to get it if we've eaten the right way all along the road to that purpose.

Good nutrition is tied in with our minds—ever heard of "brain food"? It's clearly related to bodily health. And the phrase "soul food" notwithstanding, the soul, too, is tied in with our nutrition. And how about money? Money ties in with everything. We need energy and a clear mind to earn it. And good nutrition can actually be a wise expenditure when we observe that restaurants, and the kind of food they tend to serve, are poor investments of our money if overused.

Eating well isn't nearly the burden some people think it is. In our chapter about it, we'll examine a positive plan for giving your body the kind of quality fuel it craves.

MONEY

The topic of finance couldn't be further removed from the idea of the soul. We move from the intangible to the utterly tangible; from the eternal to that which "you can't take with you."

Money can come and go in the matter of an instant, yet it provides our score-keeping in this world. Whether or not we feel it *should* do so, it's the popular perception that finance guides modern life, and that he who has the gold makes the rules.

Once again, of course, we detect the overlap with the other essentials. Can we think clearly and make the best plans when we're anxious about our finances? Do we have the full ability to care for our bodies and perhaps work out at the gym if we're flat broke? It's also clear that our relationship with money is guided by the soul and can pollute it as well.

We earn money, we spend money, and we save money. The rules seem fairly simple. So why is it that so few people master their financial situation? In this chapter, we'll talk about our relationship with money and its obvious bearing on the pursuit of a life purpose. What money actually does is provide options. To get where we want to go, we'll need to be well-financed. Without the financial foundation, we'll be caught in the cycle of paying bills and simply scrambling to stay afloat.

We'll discuss your money and your handling of it in practical applications that will help you think about where you're going and what you'll need to get there.

RELATIONSHIPS

If you think about it, we've discussed five very personal, very individual essentials: the mind and body and soul that only you have; your personal finances; what you, and no one but you, will eat. The final essential, however, pulls back the curtain and involves others. We're talking about your relationships.

The poet John Donne said, "No man is an island, entire of itself; every man is a piece of the continent." His point was that we're all connected, even in a Western culture that stresses individualism. We talk about becoming the "best version of ourselves," and that can seem like a purely personal effort—something to pursue on your own.

But as people, we're really not wired that way. The many go-getters I know are self-starters. They compete with themselves, and they're motivated by their own goals rather than any desire to keep up with someone else. Yet none of them are lone rangers. They haven't reached their level of achievement without understanding their need for others.

We know all this, of course, but we often take it for granted. We neglect those closest to us as we become wrapped up in our various pursuits. We use people rather than interact and serve them.

This final essential is all about relationships, the various categories of them, and how we can maximize them as we manifest our life purpose. Working well with others is no easy task. And once again, please know that healthy, positive relationships aren't optional. They're a part of each of the essentials we've already discussed.

In short, we're talking about six essentials, and each one must be addressed specifically and consistently. But the beautiful thing is that as you polish one, the others are also more likely to shine. For example, when we care for the body, we think more clearly. When we eat better, the body is at its best. Strong personal relationships are good for the soul. And so on.

So let's talk about a lifelong program of caring for the essentials, starting with your mind. In the next chapter, be prepared to start thinking about your thinking.

CHAPTER SIX

ESSENTIAL 1

SHARPENING THE MIND

"Our life is what our thoughts make it."

—MARCUS AURELIUS

The mind is a mysterious thing. Even the most advanced science hasn't fully explained what goes on inside our heads. We know that neurons fire through circuits called synapses. They bring us messages; they carry our responses. And we can direct the twitch of a finger, or a life-altering decision, or a moment of fantasy—any little or big task the mind carries out.

Have you ever stopped to consider and observe your thinking process? It's a little like looking at yourself in a mirror, only to see yourself looking at yourself. You'd rather see what you look like doing something else, but you can only watch yourself watching yourself. In the same way, it's hard to observe our thinking objectively.

Try this: just stop thinking completely for a moment or two.

How'd you do? I'm betting you failed. The mind really has no off switch; even when you sleep, the night shift is quietly doing its thing inside your brain. To live is to think, just as much as to breathe.

So how much thinking do you control? That's what really concerns us in this chapter. The truth is you have as much conscious control as you care to exert. You can certainly decide at any moment what to think about. Try thinking about a purple gorilla. Got that image? Good. Now, *do not* think about the purple gorilla. Kick that picture completely out of your mind. Whatever you do, *don't think about a purple gorilla.*

Yes, once the thought is there you can't *not* think about it. What you've discovered is that while your mind obeys orders, it also has a mind of its own. As a matter of fact, a lot of your thinking is purely involuntary. Whenever you're not giving your mind a specific command, it cruises where it will, like a car whose driver is asleep at the wheel. You might be sitting at home, staring out a window, or in a dull business meeting. Your mind wanders; where does it go? Where does your mind like to wander? Sports? The past? Something you'd rather not discuss?

If we inserted a little digital recorder in our brains and later read a transcript of all the day's thoughts, I imagine we'd be surprised by all the places our minds traveled—and how much of it was actually fueled by emotion or impulse or irrational thinking patterns. For example:

"I don't have enough money."

"No one listens to me."

"I'm drinking too much."

Our minds are like fine stallions. They can travel quickly, cover a lot of ground, and also carry us off course. The mind, bumped and bruised through life's setbacks and unpleasant experiences, is capable of thinking in negative, unhealthy ways. The reins are in our hands, but the horse needs to be trained and guided.

If you've suffered a business setback, been fired, or been through a divorce, negative thoughts will take residence in your thinking. And what happens if we don't break those thought habits? We layer sad or pessimistic or embittered thoughts on top of each other. Do you know anyone who has done this over a lengthy period of time? You listen to them and think, "Don't they hear themselves? Don't they realize how negative, how irrational, they sound?" We can create negative patterns of thinking that bring about negative lives.

Yet the reverse must also be true. Consider the effect of years of positive, healthy thinking. What would happen if you took time regularly to examine your thinking and the speech that proceeds from it? What if you insisted on discrediting and discarding every unhealthy thought you could detect, even asking the people you care about to help you do so?

Consider this, too. To a considerable extent, we can choose the pattern of our own thought; we can work diligently to overthrow poor thought patterns and replace them with healthy ones. Given that idea, and wanting to get your mind on the right path, what subjects would you choose to think about?

We can't be monitoring our thinking processes every second; life comes at us too quickly. But we do have opportunities to watch out for negative thoughts and to exchange them. What subjects would you like to think less about? You might want to make a two-column list with "Think about this" in one column and "Don't even think about it!" in the other.

We'll use it as a template to wrap our minds around this vast topic of human thought.

THINKING

Basic thinking, the kind we think of as intelligence, is the first area. As you went through school or simply lived your life, you learned new things all the time. You were using and growing the *cognitive* side of the brain, and always continuing to add on. As you do your regular day's thinking, making countless decisions about what to eat, how to use your time, what to talk about, and so on, you're using this basic thinking capacity.

The classic way to measure intelligence, of course, is through an IQ test (intelligence quotient), which seeks to create a measurement for our level of intelligence. There's a lot of debate about these tests, but on a basic level, an IQ test does a good job of quantifying your basic skill of thinking.

Have you ever met someone who doesn't seem to think very logically? Perhaps their decisions are agenda-based and more emotional, more biased. On the other hand, you've probably met others who think very logically and carefully rather than making snap decisions. They're likely to point out factors and issues you wouldn't have thought about—their wheels are turning all the time in their heads. These are people high in cognitive ability, and quite often, they're lower on the emotional scale. And that's just as important.

FEELING

Next there's the emotional side of our thinking. The feeling, or *affective*, side of our thoughts is far more powerful than most of us realize. In the first category, your mind basically computes. It gathers and uses facts. But on the affective side, your mind responds emotionally in your interactions. Think about someone you know who is very compassionate; someone who deeply feels not only their own pain, but the pain of others. Perhaps they're more likely to be sympathetic than judgmental.

Imagine you sit down at the dinner table and someone brings you a plate of spinach. Your cognitive mind will look at it, identify it as spinach, and perhaps tell you it's a very healthy and nutritional thing to eat. Your affective mind, however, might tell you, "I hate that kind of vegetable!" So there's one vote for healthy, one for "Yuck!"

Which voice is loudest? For most of us who are this side of *Star Trek*'s Mr. Spock, the emotions tend to win out. That's just life. Our feelings are powerful influences throughout the day—and that's why we need to use our cognitive abilities to assess them. But emotions are very fluid. Just as we continue to gather cognitive information, we continue to adjust our feelings. You might meet a new coworker and find that your feelings toward him or her change over time, for example. Or you find new ways to enjoy spinach.

IQ tests would tell us little about our feelings, but other assessments can be very helpful. The Myers-Briggs Type Indicator, for example, is a popular way to get a helpful measurement of what kind of "feeler" we may be. There are also EQ (emotional intelligence) tests that are created to measure this part of the personality.

DOING

Mental theorist Kathy Kolbe has done a great deal of work in the field of how we think, and particularly how we instinctually behave based on our thought patterns. She has developed the Kolbe A Index, which contemplates "doing" one of three basic parts of the mind: thinking, feeling, and doing. While there are many ways to define "taking action," I've found the Kolbe view to be very workable.

The third component of the mind, according to her index, is the *conative* or "doing" faculty. It's all about how we take our thoughts and feelings and connect them to our actions—projecting our thoughts to the outside world. As we've discussed, our minds are working all the time. We gather information, we think something about it and feel something about it, and then we act—or not. Behavior is the "doing" aspect of the mind.

We may not identify action with thinking, but of course, we act only based on how we've decided to respond. Conative thinking is about the will or volition. It's related to our motivations, our goals, and our intentions. And just as we have very personal cognitive and emotional styles, we also have a conative style. That is, we have preferred ways of acting, deciding, or responding that have to do with our personality framework.

Imagine you're in an office environment, you manage a few

employees, and you discover that someone on the team has been doing poor work during the current quarter. First, you come to that judgment by examining the records carefully. That's your thinking faculty, and hopefully you've used it effectively by getting all the information possible and studying it objectively. Then you may respond emotionally. You may grow angry, you may feel compassion for the worker, you may feel annoyed that it's a fire to put out, or you may simply feel mild disappointment.

But how are you going to handle it? That's the conative side, and here we can begin to see what a difference this part of the mind makes. We may have small differences in how we think and feel in such a situation, but the options for behavior are nearly infinite. You could ignore the situation and hope it goes away, because you hate confrontation. You could call in the coworker and face the issue head-on. You could take this person to lunch, ask questions, listen carefully, and give friendly, mentor-like advice. You could simply recommend this employee be liberated to the workforce. All of these options are related to behavioral styles that different people might prefer. And you can think of others. What would yours be? How would you describe your problem-solving style?

None of us would handle any given situation with precisely the same mixture of thinking, feeling, and doing. The Kolbe A Index is one test especially geared to measuring your behavioral tendencies. And again, Myers-Briggs and other such evaluations paint revealing portraits of how we're likely to act.

KNOW THYSELF

The Greek philosophers said, "Know thyself," and it's still good advice for all of us—essential for those who want to fulfill a meaningful purpose. We need to know our own minds if we plan on charting our own course.

Perhaps you already have a pretty good idea of your strengths, your weaknesses, and your general response style. You may have taken some kind of personality assessment. Tests such as the ones we've mentioned are good ways to get you thinking about how your mind works.

It's actually a liberating experience when we come to understand what makes us tick. For one thing, we're freed from guilt about what we perceive as weaknesses. We're not deficient as people; we have our strengths and we have our failings. Creative people often beat themselves up over lacking precision with details and organizational skills. But this is very common in those who think outside the box. Highly organized people may wish they were more creative. Nobody is "everything." None of us are islands, sufficient unto ourselves. We're all pieces of a continent, and we need each other. It's a wonderful day when we come to understand that and accept ourselves simply as we're wired.

Understanding the mental framework that guides us, we can design a life that makes a good fit and helps us pursue our goals. I've mentioned the first jobs I ever had, and how miserable and unsuccessful I was as, for example, a commission sales representative. As a younger man, I could have wondered what was wrong with me. After all, other people made lots of sales and earned large commissions. The job fit them like a custom-tailored suit. I sensed that I'd be stronger in other settings.

Then I took a Kolbe A assessment and finished with a score of 7, 5, 8, 2. Those numbers were ranks for the categories of Fact Finder,

Follow Through, Quick Start, and Implementer. My highest score of 8 was for Quick Start, meaning I like to jump right in and try a solution without necessarily knowing the outcome. It also means I need variety, and it perfectly explains why the entrepreneurial life was such a good fit—new things all the time, plenty of risk. I'm not the type who would work in one job for twenty years, with every day the same. Others would flourish in settings of consistency and repetition; neither should feel superior or inferior. We just have different wiring.

My Kolbe evaluation suggested I would make a good coach or a teacher, and it made perfect sense. I love working with people and explaining things. I love the experience of motivating others and seeing them figure things out. So as I learned about where I was most likely to flourish, I began thinking in terms of what kind of career would fit that, in accordance with my purpose. Purpose, profile, and passion—all in sync.

What would your life look like if you came to the best possible understanding of how your mind works and what you most wanted to achieve, then custom-designed your activities to fit? I believe that is the best path to arranging a successful and productive life.

SHARPENING YOUR TOOLS

We've talked about our mental design and the importance of accepting it. But does that mean we're limited, that we can't grow mentally as we move through life? Of course not. We've all known people who, through their own efforts, developed stronger minds. There are "self-made" men and women who lacked the best educational opportunities but read widely and grew mentally. The brain is anything but a closed system. We can feed it with knowledge and insight through reading and continuing to educate ourselves. So an easy recommendation is never to stop reading, learning, and expanding your mind.

Here are some other ideas:

⟹ **Take personality tests and other inventory assessments** such as the ones we've mentioned in this book. On our website, www.tedbradshaw.com, we offer recommendations for resources. Even if you took Myers-Briggs or some other test years ago, get a fresh take, in the light of your current thoughts on purpose. If you've never measured your EQ and explored your emotional intelligence, be sure to pay attention to that area, too. It's vital in how you interact with people, giving close attention to thinking, feeling, and doing.

⟹ **Daily journaling** is a wonderful way to organize your thoughts. It's become an absolute essential in my own daily life. I have a period in the morning to take a quick snapshot of how I'm doing in my thinking, my emotions, my ambitions, and whatever else is going on in my thoughts. I'm not talking about a diary. This is a journal that helps you think about your thinking, and to remind yourself of the mental disciplines you're working to learn.

⟹ **Meditation.** This is another helpful exercise to rest and strengthen your mind. I'm not necessarily advocating any religious view of meditation, though you may find some of those helpful. This is about simply spending a few minutes guiding your thinking in positive directions, taking a break from the grind simply to claim some margin for reflection. In the noise and chaos of our times, we spend too little time stopping, looking, and listening to our inner voices or being present in the moment.

⟹ **Evaluate your progress regularly.** Later in this book, we'll talk about strategies for regular goal-setting and self-grading. For now, simply notice. Are you wanting to become a more disciplined thinker, say, in avoiding resentful thoughts about people you work with? Write down that goal, meditate on it, include it in your journal, and then evaluate your progress a week or a month from now. You'll find this system of self-reminders will keep this goal at the forefront of your mind, and you'll be pleased with how it changes the direction of your thinking.

It's been said the mind is a terrible thing to waste, and this chapter has offered guidance on growing rather than neglecting that incredible gift that sits atop our spinal cords. After all, the mind is powerful yet fragile. It rests within a time-sensitive container known as the human body. Is there any way to expand its shelf life?

That's the next essential for our discussion.

CHAPTER SEVEN

ESSENTIAL 2

CARING FOR THE BODY

"We don't stop playing because we grow old; we grow old because we stop playing."

—GEORGE BERNARD SHAW

Mike Flynt was reminiscing with a few old friends. He couldn't help but mention his one great regret: an unfinished college football career. He thought about it by day, dreamed about it by night.

Flynt had been the best player on his college team, no doubt about it. But just before his senior season, he'd been kicked off the squad after yet another fistfight on campus. It was a bad habit, and it had cost him before. Losing that senior year, however, was a crushing blow.

Listening to his story, a buddy said, "Well, why not do something about it? Don't you still have a year of eligibility?" Flynt had a good laugh. He was fifty-nine years old!

But the seed was planted in his imagination. The idea was so insane, it just might work. He was going to do it, never mind his age. Let them laugh; he was still tough.

Sure enough, people were aghast. "You'll get yourself killed," they warned. But Flynt kept working out, toning his muscles, and finally he moved his family to West Texas. There he reenrolled at Sul Ross State University, his old school, and tried out for the football team, a grizzled face among a bunch of kids who could have been his grandchildren, and coaches who could have been his sons.

At first people laughed at the freak show. Then they were inspired. Mike Flynt had a reasonably strong season, playing regularly at linebacker and on special teams. No teammate was more hard nosed. That season made him the oldest player in NCAA football history. ESPN featured his story. *Sports Illustrated* ran it, too, and soon there was a book deal. How did the old man pull it off?

It certainly didn't hurt that he'd been a strength coach for Nebraska, Oregon, and Texas A&M. He'd invented his own fitness system. No ordinary fifty-nine-year-old body could have pulled it off. But Mike Flynt had a physique that most twenty-somethings would envy.

Few men or women take such immaculate care of their bodies. What would happen to our trillion-dollar healthcare expenses if we did? How much more productive would we all be?

THE WHOLE PACKAGE

Remember when everything came from the local mall? These days, we do a lot of our shopping online, and that makes shipping important. If you order, let's say, a new and expensive coffee machine, the last thing you want is to receive a torn and dented package with damaged merchandise inside. Packaging counts, and that holds true for everything that makes up a human being.

We've already talked about the mind, the literal brain trust of your life. We can read, study, earn degrees, and gain a lifetime of experience—but if we carry that mind in a defective package, that brain will do us little good. Most of us accept the proposition that aging degrades our physical abilities—but are we surrendering without a fight? Just how much of that degradation must we allow?

Some people give up too soon and enjoy life a lot less. Then there are the rare individuals like Mike Flynt who shows us just what could be if we nurtured and maintained the basic equipment.

Some of the life purposes we choose require many years of dedication to achieve to the fullest. To excel, to go that second and third mile, we need rested, strong, healthy physical faculties. As we'll find in every chapter, this essential affects all the others. A chain is only as strong as its weakest link. How many millionaires have done well with the financial essential, built great minds, forged strong relationships, but found that no amount of money would purchase the physical health they'd squandered?

When I go to the gym, I see a lot of young men and women. They already possess the advantages of youth—their bodily "packages" are undented, untorn—but they're interested in making those bodies stronger, leaner. Some of it may be ego; they may want that beach body.

As we grow older, however, there's more of a sense of urgency.

We're fighting the battle of the bulge; our muscle mass is decreasing. The mirror is one source of motivation for getting in shape. I've also seen a lot of people who need some kind of race or competition as an incentive—a triathlon, a marathon, an after-work softball league, or a tennis rival. And some of us simply enjoy a good, brisk workout.

Whatever the motivation, a session at the gym is going to be beneficial, as long we go through it safely. What we want to discuss here is the need for body care as it relates to being energetic and productive in fulfilling our purpose in the world, with as few physical limitations as possible.

What was your reaction when you saw the present subject matter? Was it, "Bring it on! I'm in a good place with my fitness." Or maybe you groaned; you hate running and working out. You'd rather read a book than ride a bike. Physical fitness is not your thing.

We're not talking about becoming superstar athletes or winning weight-lifting contests. None of that is necessary for the routine maintenance that leads to a healthy, fit body. And good health, as we'll all agree, pays no end of dividends in contentment and success in life.

EXERCISE AND THE MIND

Those who enjoy running will tell you about "runner's high," those moments of euphoria that come across them once they get going. It's an obvious example of the deep links between our physical and mental worlds. Intense exercise releases endorphins into the blood. That's nature's way of giving you a nice rush of pure and healthy happiness.

But that's not the only perk exercise provides for your mental state. Studies show that physical exertion is good for anxiety, depression, and stress. But most of us have already experienced this, haven't we? When we have a case of the blues, we actually feel a lack of energy, so we're more likely to mope around the house. A good, vigorous walk out in the sunshine can have a near-miraculous effect. Somehow the anxiety eases up, at least a bit. Problems don't seem so massive out in the sunshine or while you're working up a good sweat at the gym.

Exercise promotes plenty of healthy brain activity: neural growth, cerebral changes that promote feelings of calmness, and again, endorphin releases. There's also a simple common sense advantage: a busy, active body is distracted from negative thinking. Unhealthy thinking patterns are disrupted.

Depression isn't the only thing that gives a little when you exercise. I work with quite a few executives these days who struggle with the symptoms of attention deficit hyperactivity disorder. Physical activity provides a dopamine boost in the brain, which is the most prominent chemical messenger of pleasure. Serotonin levels are also increased, and these are good for focus and attention.

The greatest mental benefit of all may be energy. Big ideas require stamina and staying power. As you go through life, become smarter and wiser, and grow wider-canvas ideas and ambitions, what a shame it is to be limited by a dwindling energy supply. A lethargic body leads to lethargic thinking. The connections between the body and the mind are tight in every way.

I have to admit my bias as someone who has enjoyed exercise all my life. For me, physical exercise and competition have always been associated with healthy thinking and quality of life. I'm at my best when I've given my body the good workout it always craves. I can't imagine anything else. I enjoyed competitive hockey from childhood on, until it was time to move on to other things. I found triathlons and, for a good while, I was tremendously motivated to compete in that field. But the time came when I was ready to move on from that, too, and I got into other kinds of sports.

But that's just me. I had a colleague whose thing was salsa dancing. That was the mode of exercise that appealed to her, and she made it work.

I'll be into exercise as long as I'm physically capable of it, and of course that's enhanced by simply staying fit. A healthy body is good for a healthy mind, and a healthy mind makes it easier for me to have the discipline to maintain my health.

Yet I know exercise isn't number one on everyone's playlist. I want to encourage people to call that mindset into question. But rather than appeal to guilt or fear, I'd rather present some of the incredible benefits of taking care of your body, other than the simple reality that it's the only carrying case we'll ever have.

Let's examine four major areas of body care.

CARDIO

Cardiovascular capability is the body's ability to process oxygen, which gives us the ability to move. The cardiovascular system is heart, blood vessels, and blood. That system transports oxygen all across your body. If you're going to climb a set of stairs, cardio conditioning helps you do that without a strain. If you need to slow down your heart rate and your breathing after a little physical exertion, cardio helps. Then we can put our energy to other uses. And simply going for a good, brisk walk helps you with your cardio.

People are realizing this. As you drive through neighborhoods, you see people of all ages out walking. Have you noticed that you rarely see any of them looking stressed or unhappy? Maybe they're intent, keeping up their pace, or with the dog on the leash, or listening to their music. But most of the time, they're at peace. They'll tell you it's their favorite time of the day, and perhaps their healthiest.

A long walk is an example of aerobic conditioning. It's all about going longer distances at lower intensity. That gives us one series of benefits, and it's not necessary to be in peak condition to get in a healthy walk.

There's also anaerobic conditioning, the high-intensity threshold approach for working out. Done correctly with appropriate guidance, even the beginner or aging adult can exercise this way, and it's a great complement to aerobic conditioning. I still play hockey twice a week. Some people simply prefer pushing themselves and working up a little more sweat.

Any type of exercise must be taken up wisely. A balanced workout routine should include doing some form of cardio three times a week. But I have a friend who runs the Boston Marathon—she can run every single day with no problem. It all depends on the person and their fitness level.

It's good to have a routine that's well thought out, but also to realize that you'll ultimately plateau if you continue to do the same thing week after week. That's when you need to change it up some, perhaps switch to a different form of exercise, something new and challenging. It might be helping you a bit less physically at that point, and you, along with your muscles, may become a little complacent.

The key is always the enjoyment you derive, because if you're not having a pleasant experience, you won't persevere. So part of the wisdom of arranging your regimen is to do what you love. For me, variety is all-important. I love mountain biking, road biking, paddleboarding, or just a nice, thoughtful hike. Another benefit that touches on the essential of relationships: you can do all these things with your friends, even business associates. Exercise is a bonding experience socially.

STRENGTH

A lot of men and women enjoy strength programs, because they're goal-oriented and competitive, and because it feels good to be stronger. There are any number of programs such as CrossFit, Orangetheory, HIIT workouts, circuit training, and others. These come and go, and again, it's simply important to find the one that fits you and your lifestyle and strength training objectives.

Strength training is more than weight lifting. In the old days, the image of this practice was having a set of barbells in the garage. Today it's become much more sophisticated and diverse, and it's all about dynamic exercise of every major muscle group in the body, with the goal of improving physical performance.

As young adults, a lot of us lift in an ego-driven way. We want the six-pack abs and the impressive biceps, and it's all about how we look in our bathing suits. As we grow older, of course, that angle is a bit less pressing, and lifting grows more difficult.

Some people put less emphasis on strength at this stage—why should they worry about how many pounds they can bench? But strength still needs to be incorporated into the workout. Appearance was never really the best reason for strength conditioning anyway. We begin to lose muscle mass as early as our twenties. We want to maintain and even increase bone density. We don't want our joints to begin deteriorating. There are a great many benefits to full-body strength workouts.

But do you need weights? Do you have to have access to all that machinery at the gym? Simply do an online search, and you'll find all kinds of ways to do strength conditioning at home, and with ordinary things: a chair; a doorway; the floor, if you do simple push-ups. You might be surprised at the quality of workout you can get without any equipment whatsoever. And while it's not necessary to use a strength coach, it's important to be sure we're using proper form. The last thing we want is to damage our backs or otherwise cause injury. If you haven't been involved with strength conditioning, do your research and start simply. Do some basic exercises at home, or get some coaching at the gym. Have some fun with it, and feel the burn!

MOBILITY

As we grow older, mobility may be the most important of the three areas of health we've discussed—and the most neglected. These are abilities to move and stretch that we possess on a "use it or lose it" basis.

Mobility is simply the ability to move about freely and easily, and something we take for granted when we're younger. As children, we may not have much muscular strength, and our cardio may need development, but our mobility is off the charts. Children are incredibly flexible. But the longer we live, the more of that begins to fade. And as we lose some of this functionality, the body compensates. It finds a way for you to make that stretch or move that joint, and these work-arounds lead to muscles up and down the kinetic chain working extra, or out of their normal range—and the final result is pain and injury.

It's not really a matter of muscle loss, or the ability to run up a flight of stairs. You're going to feel it through joint pain in the knees and elbows. Your hips will begin to give you problems. We need to keep our muscles long and lean through the years, and our tendons stretched, to hold off some of those aches and pains that close in on us with advancing years.

It's not difficult at all to do exercises for mobility, and these exercises can be done in a few minutes in the morning or just before going to bed. That kind of habit makes all the difference. On top of that, once or twice a week, more intentional mobility exercises such as yoga or Pilates can be powerful disciplines as well.

In my schedule, it works to do my exercises for forty-five to sixty minutes about an hour after waking up. I need to get my blood pumping and my muscles awake for the new day before I approach my little ritual. After a good set of stretching and mobility exercises, I'm more than ready to take on whatever is before me.

Again, you don't need special equipment or guidance, though of course, you'll find some good coaching at the gym. You'll want to take special care to be safe and cautious. There are a great number of good exercise sites on the internet, and you can watch videos there, showing you exactly how to get a good range of motion with all your movements.

I guarantee, your body will greatly appreciate it. I can remember a two-year period of serious back problems, one of the worst trials I've ever endured. I couldn't do my cardio or strength workouts, I couldn't sleep well, and the difference was all too apparent in my state of mind, which was far less positive. It was my focus on mobility, however, that pulled me through.

If you're going to work on these various functions, use alternating days to attend to each. You might have a strength day, then a cardio day, while working on mobility for a few minutes each morning or evening. Don't be haphazard in your workouts, but use a well-thought-out plan to concentrate on different muscle groups on appropriate days. And many of the experts will advise us to limit the number of high-intensity training sessions per week. We might feel we're pushing ourselves "to the max," but the body has its limits, and we can actually do a good bit of damage by overdoing it.

SLEEP

This one is a late-breaking addition to my list. Originally I listed cardio, strength, and mobility as the three areas of bodily health I wanted to discuss. But more and more, I began to notice the vast importance of sleep, and the problem it's become for so many people. I came to the conclusion that sleep is as important as any other item on the list.

We don't think of sleep in relation to cardio and the others, because it's the opposite of physical exercise and workouts. It's rest. But rest, of course, is an essential part of the equation. Most of us feel we don't need any help in learning how to rest, but without realizing it, we may actually be deficient in the art of a good night's sleep. And if you're working out several times a week, you need sleep even more, so that your body can make use of that downtime to recover and rebuild.

Sleep attends to a lot of bodily tasks we don't even realize. When we've been exposed to a flu virus or a cold virus, sleep is the simplest and often best defense the body has. It strengthens the immune system. Lack of sleep allows all kinds of "invaders," bacterial and otherwise, to breach our defenses.

The research tells us that seven to eight hours of sleep per night should be the goal. We hear of people who need much less sleep, but that's a rarity. We need to start with making sure we know that we're going to bed in time to get those eight hours, ideally, before it's time to rise in the morning.

And what about the quality of our sleep? There are actually many steps we can take to improve our sleep to get as much deep rest as possible. An hour to two hours before bedtime, there should be no more screens—television, computer, any kind of screen. Studies are telling us that the light emitted from these screens disrupts the brain's process of going into sleep mode. I've used a screen filter for my tablet, but the latest research suggests I may need to rethink that, too. Best simply to stay away from screens.

Consider picking up a book. Reading provides a gentle, restful workout for the mind before bedtime. The right subject matter will place your thoughts in a positive zone just when they should be there. Screens—TV and computers—are to be avoided. Watching the news at night is a bad idea because of the emotions those subjects can stir up. And research shows us that the artificial light from these screens is detrimental to our brains beginning to shut down in preparation for rest.

Midnight snacks? Also a bad idea. I don't eat once the clock is ticking down to three hours before I go to bed. Let the body get ahead on digestion, and you'll rest better.

Some people take medicinal sleeping aids. Sometimes, during a difficult stretch, these may be helpful, but in the long run, they're not the best idea; they create dependencies, and they bring us within a step of prescribed sleeping pills. Those can be addictive. Better options are relaxing music, meditation, reflection, and a well-designed room for sleeping; everything around you should be related to calm and getting a good sleep. The room should be tidy and relaxing in appearance. The reason many of us enjoy hotels so much is that the rooms are cleaner, simpler, calmer, and well-designed for sleep.

I find that when I do all these things, I don't need an alarm clock. My body understands the rhythms of my life, and it gently awakens me at the right time. I think we can all agree that a gentle mental prompt is better than the sound of an alarm, or sudden music or talking that shocks us awake.

You might have noticed we have some great technology to help us with our sleep. I wear a special ring (Oura) that tracks vital statistics and rates my sleep, and there are watches that offer all kinds of health information. Being a competitive guy, I love keeping up with my best and worst nights of sleep. The record motivates me to improve my habits even more. In case you're curious, my worst night was scored a forty-two on a scale of one to one hundred, and I could have told you exactly why—a bad combination of elements. My best night ever was a score of ninety-four, and that was an evening when I followed all the advice in this section perfectly. I'm always trying to set a new record and, more importantly, be consistent.

Most of us would be shocked at how much better we would think and feel if we simply took the steps to getting a better night's sleep, and getting it consistently. Good sleep is the missing link to a better life for so many people today, and they're beginning to realize it. Have you noticed all the TV advertisements for mattresses and pillows? Have you noticed the attention given to the problem of sleep apnea? The growing "sleep aid" section at the local pharmacy?

Lack of sleep is an epidemic, but there are so many simple and practical steps we can take to confront the problem. It's also a good idea to see a qualified sleep doctor if you do suffer from sleep apnea or some issue that's a bit larger than what we've discussed.

* * *

As you think back over this chapter, which of the four main sections caught your attention the most? In which area(s) do you most need to make changes?

It would be a mistake simply to turn the page and keep reading without stopping to begin working on a plan. All of us could do a better job caring for these vessels that transport us through the voyage of life. I'm working all the time to do a better job with mine. I highly recommend creating a full week's routine for good, well-rounded exercise and sleep. It's okay to begin small, with just a few well-chosen items. You'll experience more peace of mind and rest, not only for your body but for your soul.

Speaking of which—we take a sharp turn in the next chapter and talk about that strange, controversial, and hidden part of who we are: the soul.

CHAPTER EIGHT

ESSENTIAL 3

DEEPENING THE SOUL

"Before all it's necessary to look after the soul, if you want the head and the rest of the body to function correctly."

—PLATO

The best stories never grow old. They're simply updated to match their times and places. Take the fairy tale "Cinderella"—it doesn't really need castles, princes, or fairy godmothers; you can place that story in any setting. The basic message is what matters, and it never wears out.

Or consider the legend of Faust, the story of a man willing to sell his soul to the Devil for worldly gain. "Devil's bargain" stories have always been around. The Broadway musical *Damn Yankees* is a version of the Faust story—this time in the world of baseball!

But what exactly is so timeless about the idea of selling a soul? It's at least as old as a Bible verse: "For what is a man profited, if he shall gain the whole world, and lose his own soul? or what shall a man give in exchange for his soul?" (Matthew 16:26) There it is: the idea that we have something called a soul, and even more interestingly—that it can be lost! Something there touches a nerve; we believe the soul is precious and to be cherished.

But wait. What *is* the soul? It can't be found in human anatomy. There's no home, no substance, no real *function* that we can specify. The soul is defined as the immaterial essence of a human being. People of all cultures and creeds have agreed there's something in us that transcends the here and now. In general, we speak of the soul as that part of us that is eternal.

We've talked about the mind and the body, thoughts and emotions. But these don't tell the whole story of who we are, do they? What is that thing within us that seeks meaning, that senses right and wrong, that looks to the infinite, that responds to nature, art, and music? And who's that inside you—that essential, authentic you, when you're alone and fully yourself? World religions have their own unique ways of explaining all this. Philosophers continue to debate the questions we've raised. But for our purposes here, it's enough to recognize there's something unique and individual in us, something we identify as the soul.

If that's true, then it's another part of us that needs attention as we seek to fulfill our purpose in life. But how, exactly, do you improve a soul? Reading philosophy? Doing good deeds? Religious affiliation?

I spent some time thinking and reading about the soul, particularly on the question of where we can all agree, across the differences of religion or even without involving religion. I began with the idea that the mind is our navigation system for the journey we're describing. The body is the vessel that takes us there. And the soul? It's the propulsion system. It empowers us in a way nothing else can. If you're traveling by water, you can exert yourself and row the boat—and tire out pretty quickly—*or* you can have a powerful engine and go the distance.

The soul is the powerful engine that gives power and resonance to our ideas, our energy, our depth of commitment. We have an intrinsic need to look at life and find within it meaning and significance. In Faustian terms, there needs to be something about us, something within us, that we wouldn't trade even for all the world's wealth. And it's our essential selves. This I believe.

My next question was, how can I wrap my arms around this idea of the soul? What, if any, details could I use to describe it more closely? This is where ancient Greek philosophy came to my rescue.

PLATO AND THE SOUL

Plato is considered the father of Western philosophy. He was quite interested in the human soul, or *psyche*, in the Greek language. As he saw it, there were three parts to the soul:

⟹ **The rational, or the mind.** Plato's meaning isn't to be confused with what we discussed as "the mind" in our previous chapter. We were talking about our basic thinking abilities and intelligence. For Plato, the rational soul is our conscious awareness. In an analogy of his time, he called it the charioteer who holds the reins of the horses, guiding them along. He thinks, analyzes, plans his turns, and uses logic to make the best journey to his destination. Again, this is not our basic logic, but *our soul's logic.* Plato may not have made this fine distinction, but for my purposes, the rational soul makes ethical decisions, guiding us based on what we truly believe.

➡ **The spirited** part of the soul. This is the part that may get angry, perhaps at the sight of injustice or cheating or the flourishing of evil. When we see a child being bullied on a playground, for example, we react emotionally. This is the soul using our emotional faculties. It's also the competitive streak many of us have—the love of challenges, the drive to win honor or to distinguish ourselves. We're not just thinking logically and rationally, but with *soul,* and with an emotional approach to what is important in life. Returning to the chariot, Plato describes a white horse and a dark horse pulling the vehicle. He identifies the spirited soul with the noble white horse.

➡ **The appetites,** which are the body's drives for comfort, pleasure, sensation, and physical satisfaction. You might not predict these urges to be part of the soul, but Plato identified them with the dark horse, the impulsive one. That horse is a bit headstrong and unpredictable. Plato pointed out that these appetites can fight each other and fight the other parts of the soul. You see a fattening dessert on the menu, and your rational brain quickly tells you it's not part of your new, healthy body goals. But the appetite wants what it wants. It tugs at the reins and says, "Let's go! Just do it!" Desire is quite often a good thing. We have appetites for love and acceptance, for beauty, for fine things. But as we all know, desire isn't always the best guide.

Please know that Plato offers one template for understanding the human soul; there are countless others. In this book, we're dealing with a great many disciplines of science, psychology, philosophy, and other areas. Our strategy is to keep things simple and basic, because all of those are simply aspects of the journey of purpose. I adopt Plato's concept because it's as good as any other to help us wrap our arms around the idea of the soul.

GETTING TO KNOW OUR SOUL

Plato said there's a rational, a spirited, and an appetite-driven way to behave. So the primarily rational types, he concluded, should run the government. They think logically and unemotionally, so let them make the big decisions. Then the spirited people, who are more gung ho and who respond emotionally to injustice, should be soldiers. And finally, he associated appetites with the common people. I suppose they're "consumers"!

This was all, of course, in the context of his simpler, less scientific world. I also think he was making a particular point, not seriously suggesting people have only one flavor of soul. Each of us is rational, spiritual, *and* appetite-driven. There aren't three kinds of people in the world; there are countless kinds. If we're approaching the soul as the essence of who we are as individuals, then it follows that we each have some blend of soulful characteristics that define us.

What I want to suggest is that, as we grow as people, and discover who we're meant to be and what we're meant to do, we need to be self-aware. We must know ourselves, decide what we believe about life and the universe, and live in accordance with that. It's not enough to simply say, "I don't care about anything but pursuing pleasure or the next paycheck." We're more than that, and to fulfill a meaningful purpose, we have to nurture the soul.

From the perspective of Plato's idea, we can make *better, more rational decisions* based on who we are. We can use our *high spirits and emotional responses* in the right areas, in accordance with our soul. And we can control our *appetites*, using them in positive ways—relating to food, sex, and other forms of pleasure—in the understanding of what this life is all about. In all these ways, we deepen the soul.

Some readers may say, "I was with you until this chapter. I don't know about this soul business. It's all too speculative. You go ahead and power through this one, and I'll meet you in the next chapter." But is that an option? What risks are we running when we neglect the soul, enigmatic as it may be?

We need only check the latest news feed on our phones. Think about what's happening in business and government, where we find leaders who seem to lack values. How many people out there are guided strictly by appetite, and where does that lead them? How many are high-spirited politically, without tempering the crusade with thoughtful logic? There's not much talk about the soul of a nation or a culture, but once we think about it—its presence or absence becomes clear. Again, where's the profit if we lose our soul?

The subject may be a difficult one, but that's simply another reason to think deeply about it.

THE SOUL AT WAR

Think of these three aspects: rational, spirited, and appetites. Through all that we do and decide, they're in dialogue. In the moment, which one guides the decision? The soul moderates the dialogue, balancing them. Its goal is always its idea of ultimate meaning. We need balance between the rational, the spirited, and our desires as we navigate our journey through the labyrinth of life. Otherwise, with the soul out of balance or at war between its three sides, we'll choose poor pathways. The stronger and better-defined the soul, the more effectively it will guide that "discussion."

For example, without mature use of the rational side, our perceptions will be overwhelmed by emotion and appetite in our decision-making. I think about the cautionary tale of Bernie Madoff, the financier who'd experienced success at the highest level of his profession. He'd been the chairman of NASDAQ. Yet his appetite for more, more, more led him into nearly $65 billion worth of fraud, and he ended up in prison. Where was the soul?

Other times the rational overwhelms the spirited. Let's say we hear about an old friend who has suffered some kind of misfortune. Instead of feeling deep compassion and a powerful desire to help, we only think, "I should keep out of it. Helping might cost me time or money."

There are infinite possibilities for what could happen when the soul is out of balance. Again, just looking around us at our world gives us all the evidence we need.

On the other hand, knowing what we believe, whether through religious faith, a well-developed life philosophy, or simply a spiritual reverence for the universe, will allow us to develop depth in belief and character. The soul informs our decisions in keeping with a deeper wisdom. As an individual, you may be working from one of the common world religions, or from a mindset that is uniquely yours. The importance is in the growth you experience.

We all need some deeper point of reference in acknowledging that we're more than simple organisms, more than colliding atoms—we are more significant than that. And even so, there's something larger than ourselves. So we take up the quest to decide what that something is, and to gain whatever wisdom from it can be found. Growth of the soul is our hope to live a life of wisdom and personal consistency.

What can we do to pursue that growth? We'll examine three disciplines that have helped me profoundly as I've sought to nurture the soul within me.

MINDFULNESS

The idea of mindfulness began as a religious and a psychological concept, and it's spread in popularity to a point that we now hear about a "mindfulness movement." If this concept is new to you, it's all about being fully present in the moment, giving all our attention to that, without analyzing or any of the usual mental processes that take us out of the moment and into the maze of thinking.

Books such as *Wherever You Go, There You Are,* by Jon Kabat-Zinn, offer guidance and encouragement for us to let go of all the excess brooding, worrying, wondering, and anticipating, and instead to give all of ourselves to what's right in front of us at that very moment.

Know the importance of where you are and what is transpiring. Be aware of what you see, hear, smell, and feel—and in particular, accept that moment and resist the temptation to try and change it. Wherever you go, there you are. Don't judge yourself any more than you judge anyone or anything else. In other words, no "I wonder if I ought to be at that other place, doing that other thing? I'm behind on my deadline. I wonder if this friend or that coworker is angry with me." Give your mind a little "fresh air" by living in the moment.

It's not that you don't take responsibility. Those concerns will have their proper time and place. Right now, however, is a moment you'll never have again. It's a gift. Exercise what Eckhart Tolle calls *The Power of Now* in his book of that title. The past is old news; the future is up the road. All we have is the moment we inhabit, and the question is what we'll do with it.

I've talked to a lot of people who have discovered mindfulness. In general, they've spoken of a positive and profound spiritual effect. They're sharper, too, with more understanding of what's going on in front of them, because they're simply more attentive. They listen better. They remember better. Somebody once said that 80 percent of life is just showing up; maybe we could add that it's being *all in* where we do show up. That's good for the soul.

It's also been demonstrated that anxiety and depression decrease in the lives of mindful people, who are engaged with the now rather than brooding over the why or the what if. I would encourage you to read about mindfulness and try some of the practical exercises that are offered in the better books on that subject.

The great thing about this discipline is you can always try it *without delay.* Try it now: put down the book, look around you, listen deeply, and appreciate this tiny, present moment in time.

REFLECTION

We could say that mindfulness is *externalizing.* That is, it pulls our attention outward to what's happening all around us in that time and that space. But there are also times for deeper, more private introspection. These tend to come in the quiet times and places of life. I've chosen *reflection* as a catch-all term that might include a number of mental exercises, such as meditation, prayer, or reflection itself.

Many years ago, a question was asked of a group of people who were all at least ninety-five years old: "If you had life to live all over again, what would you do differently?" The three answers that predominated were: reflect more; risk more; and do more things that will live on after I'm gone. All of these answers are fascinating, because they reflect the wisdom of people who have journeyed through life. According to them, here were the most important things they should never have neglected.

And among those, "reflect more" might be the most compelling. It took reflection simply to answer the question, and their wish was that they'd spent more time doing that *all along*. Who among us wouldn't like to go back to some happy moment in time and simply breathe it all in once more? To take a moment to appreciate the meaning of things? Another way of saying it is, "Stop and smell the roses." Realize the goodness while it's in your grasp.

It's also a matter of thinking more deeply about where we are in life. I reflect and meditate each morning. That period of solitude and deeper thought anchors me for everything I'll do later that day. It refreshes my priorities and helps me stop to appreciate the good things going on in my life.

Reflection is simply being more thoughtful, and on a higher plane than the superficial levels on which we expend most of our conscious thoughts. We need to reflect more on marriage, on parenting, on friendships, and even when there's no crisis going on in any of the above. We need simply to be thankful and remind ourselves to have a good day.

Meditation and prayer are both excellent practices to support reflection. **Meditation** is more concentrated than reflection or mindfulness. It seeks a relaxed yet aware state, often through the repetition of a word or concept.

There are many great resources online to help someone get started in meditation. Here are six easy steps to begin the practice of meditation:

1. Find a quiet place where you won't be disturbed, and sit upright in a chair with your feet on the floor and hands on your lap.
2. Breathe deeply in through the nose and out through the mouth, with eyes open for several breaths.
3. Close your eyes and notice the space around you. Sounds, smells, feeling of the air.
4. Bring your attention to your breath, and count each inhale and exhale to ten. Then start again for several rounds.
5. Let go of the focus on the breath and the counting, and let the mind do whatever it wants to do for a minute or two.
6. Bring your attention back to the space around you and open your eyes.

The whole practice can take three minutes to three hours. Block out a little time and give it a try.

Prayer is talking to God, and if a higher power is part of your belief system, it's essential for you. Prayers can be offered in many styles. They can be offered as simple conversation with God, or readings, for example, from the Psalms or the Book of Common Prayer; they can be more creative, using imagery, for instance. There are forms of prayer that blend meditation and contemplation skills.

For me, prayer is extremely important, but you might choose one of the other disciplines we've discussed. All of these practices are accessible to everyone. All are healthy practices for the well-being of the soul.

COMMUNITY

The word *community* comes from the root word for *common*, and it's all about people who share something in common. In many traditions—community is at the very center of what it means to be human. The final of our six essentials is about the importance of people and relationships, but this question is also a matter of the soul.

We don't tend to think of the soul in social terms. After all, the soul is the very entity that makes you who you are, that is, *separate* from anyone else. No one else shares your soul—even if we're talking about your "soulmate." But the truth is that for our souls to grow, we need one another. We are not independent, self-existent creations. We're mutually dependent in every way, and as iron sharpens iron, our souls develop and differentiate themselves as they rub up against each other.

Think of all the people, beginning with your parents, who have contributed to your personal, emotional, mental, physical, and spiritual growth. That beloved schoolteacher who encouraged and inspired you? She shared from her soul. The hockey coach who taught me about mental toughness and perseverance through the many hours I spent with him? That was soul work from a man who probably never considered it that way.

But what we're really talking about here is our deep need, as adults, to be part of some kind of soulful community. I'm talking about more than just a loose affiliation of people in a club. It should be a group of people who are committed to each other, who invest time in friendship and camaraderie together, and who share some form of common belief or vision. For me, several organizations, as well as a small Bible group, serve that purpose; for others, it could be a church, synagogue, mosque, or other association; but it also could be something entirely different, something less religious.

Soul development happens when we maintain and nurture close relationships—the kind, for example, in which others can hold us accountable and speak truth into our lives; where we could share our deepest hopes and dreams; where we have serious discussions rather than superficial conversations. Such things couldn't happen at the neighborhood block party in most cases. They don't happen at the office watercooler or the gym locker room.

We need a community of fellow souls sharing a common journey. Where is yours?

* * *

What are your reflections, having thought deeply on the question of the soul? I find a wide variety of responses when I share this information in the groups I work with. For some, this is a perfectly natural topic in any discussion of a better life. Usually these are people who have some sort of religious belief, so they've been engaged at the level of the soul. It's nothing new for them.

There are others who aren't involved with traditional religion of any type. They may have walked away from that, or they may simply have never shared the most common religious beliefs. But they do resonate with the word "spiritual," they understand they possess a soul, and they get it: this is an important dynamic of life. For them, it need not be a religious one.

Finally, there are some who simply haven't thought in terms of the soul. Maybe it's the fact that we can't prove one exists, and doesn't seem to fit in with the sciences; maybe the term is too associated with beliefs they don't have. For those, this chapter may have been a challenge. My recommendation is to think carefully about the ideas here. Try some of the practices we've recommended. Whether we call the essential spirit of who you are the soul or something else—there *is* an essential you, and it wants to breathe and grow and manifest itself in the world. That's just another way of saying we all want to be all that we can be—mind, body, and soul.

CHAPTER NINE

ESSENTIAL 4

IMPROVING YOUR NUTRITION

"Let food be thy medicine and medicine be thy food."

—HIPPOCRATES

"Let's just order a pizza."

We've all said it. Dinnertime approaches; stomachs are growling. Leftovers from the fridge don't seem appealing; no one feels like cooking. And suddenly the idea of a hot, steaming pizza, with all the right ingredients and cooked by other hands, is tantalizing. That's why pizza delivery has been a growth industry for half a century.

But what if you wanted a hamburger? Or a fajita, or sushi? Until the last few years, there weren't a whole lot of delivery options for other varieties of cuisine. Then, just as services such as Uber Eats, Grubhub, and DoorDash were stepping up to supply that demand, an X factor emerged, and it changed everything: COVID-19.

The pandemic all but shut down the restaurant industry for the better part of eighteen months. The effect on food delivery was easy to anticipate. Meal delivery was the right option at the right time. As people sheltered in place, they indulged in what small comforts they could, including comfort food. Almost overnight, any restaurant wanting to stay in business had to get in on the delivery bandwagon.

But grocery shopping was affected, too: studies showed consumers buying more snacks and ready-to-eat meals. If people had to shelter in place, they were at least going to stock that shelter with the things they loved eating. Premium ice cream sales leaped, as you'd expect. We began to hear the phrase "COVID 15," referring to the fifteen pounds people were expecting to gain while staying at home. A Harvard study of fifteen million subjects and their weight changes investigated that claim. It concluded that 39 percent of its subjects gained weight during the pandemic, defined as at least two and a half pounds. Ten percent gained more than twelve and a half pounds, and 2 percent gained more than 27.5 pounds! Simply changing the types of foods people consumed surely had a drastic effect on their waistlines, and thus their health.

But the Harvard study also suggested that a significant number of people actually lost weight during the quarantine. How? Why? These were cases of people prioritizing their health by cooking healthier meals at home. While there are many people who let circumstances control their decisions, wiser heads manage their circumstances with the right decisions.

We tend to have more control than we think. "Comfort food," for example, is a choice; no one forces us to eat that jelly doughnut. Ordering out, but ordering a healthy meal, is also a choice. We prioritize the concerns that really matter to us. If we want to be healthy, there are always actions we can take to work toward that goal.

Dietary choice is the surest route to good health—or the opposite. This book is about a focused life, for people who yearn for significance and see themselves as something more than the sum of their molecular structure. By now, you know I truly believe everyone on this planet has a unique purpose, that nobody's life lacks value and potential. But how can we fulfill our purpose to the utmost if we don't care for the vessels that contain us? Our greatest dreams and ambitions are captive to these fragile bodies.

We've discussed physical body care in a past chapter, but one factor of that—the food factor—deserves a chapter all its own. Earlier, we looked at the key aspects of a healthy body—strength, cardio, mobility, and sleep. Now it's time to explore the fuel that powers your body.

PREMIUM-GRADE FUEL

I've always appreciated the place of exercise and fitness in my life, but over the years, I've come to a far deeper respect for how much of my body's fitness is determined by how I eat. When I eat the way I should, my body appreciates that decision. It expresses its appreciation by giving me energy and mental clarity. I actually find that the more I eat right, the more I want to eat right, because, well, it feels good to feel good.

Studies are showing that we really are what we eat. Food impacts mood, for example. Three different studies have suggested a direct correlation between spicy foods and aggression. It was thought to be an old myth that certain foods went along with being hot-tempered, but sure enough, careful research showed a direct causation. More generally, eating right nurtures the body and mind, so we're less likely to be anxious or depressed when our food habits are on track.

I'm careful about my diet. I can reward myself with a treat here and there, but if I let my diet slip more than just a little bit and I dump too much "cheap fuel" into this machine, my body has a reaction to that, too. It lets me know; I lose a little energy. I'm less sharp. My body is saying, "What's up? Give me the good stuff!"

We choose the right food so we can operate these bodies efficiently and carry the energy we need to perform. There's a lot of discussion today about nutrition, and particularly a surplus of competing diet fads and eating strategies. A recent *Forbes* magazine listed a few of the more popular diets of the moment: volumetrics, keto, vegan, flexitarian, raw food, probiotics, intermittent fasting.

My observation, in talking with people from many walks and stages of life, is that diet is a topic of complexity and discouragement. We struggle with our weight for some of the reasons I've mentioned, but there are others as well. Our generation is more sedentary than our ancestors were. We take in more calories than we expend, and they mount up. Then, when we try the latest diet, it works until it doesn't. Yet we know all the while that if there were an easy and lasting fix there wouldn't be a $300 billion diet industry.

Pills raise more questions: what are we putting into our bodies, anyway? And can a meal substitute meet all the vitamin and nutritional requirements of real, genuine food? Let's say the pills or the shakes help us; they may do that, for a while. What happens when we stop that regimen and go back to regular eating? Our previous selves will hurry back, unless and until our habits change. It's been demonstrated time and time again that fad diets are temporary bypasses for our habits. They don't solve the problem, and they may even make things worse.

The theme of this chapter, eating right, is a familiar one, yet one that may initially provoke a deep sigh of resignation. Hear me out. My objective in this chapter is not to lecture or restate arguments you've already heard, but to simplify this whole complex issue of nutrients and how they affect the body; to offer the simplest explanation rather than one more formula; and to encourage a healthy relationship with eating, which, more than anything else, will help us make progress that will last.

To that end, I spoke to a master dietician and nutritionist and asked her how I should organize my thoughts on this subject. I said, "Loreen, how should I simplify this whole subject of food for my readers? They've had enough fingers wagging at them—I want to keep it encouraging and accessible."

She launched into what seemed like a whole other language, filled with scientific names and processes. I was forced to stop her: "Hold up, please! Is there any way you can bring that down about ten levels of complexity?"

She laughed and said, "Sure—macros and micros." And she went on to tell me about the *macronutrients*, the nutrients our bodies need in large quantities. These are the carbohydrates, the proteins, and the fats, which provide the body with energy. Then she told me about the *micronutrients* that we need in smaller amounts: vitamins and minerals. I told her I could handle that—and that I felt our readers could, too.

Loreen offered me an entry-level view of the vast world of nutrition: carbs, proteins, fats, vitamins, and minerals. If you've found yourself overwhelmed by the maze of food information, or perhaps placed on a guilt trip by those who guilt-trip us about this subject, the simple basics in this chapter will help bring the truth out into the light, where it's not quite as frightening. And we'll discover that eating right can be enjoyable and encouraging, along with all the obvious health benefits.

MACRO- AND MICRONUTRIENTS

Nutrition is simply the process by which an organism uses food to support its life. Your body needs food regularly, daily, for survival and also for growth, development, and efficiency. Macro- and micronutrients are the components of food that your body needs.

What's the difference? Macro, of course, means *large*. Your body needs large amounts of the macronutrients—carbohydrates, proteins, and fat. All your energy comes from these, and that energy is measured in calories. In case you're curious, a calorie is how much energy is required to raise the temperature of water by one degree Celsius. I'm sure I must have learned that in high school biology.

The nutrients you need in small amounts are the micronutrients: vitamins and minerals. These two sets of energy and growth providers cooperate to help your body run just the way it should.

Carbs. Carbohydrates are found in fruits, grains, and vegetables.

They give us the sugars, starches, and fibers we need. These are the best source for quick energy, because your system can easily break them down into glucose, which helps the muscles and the brain.

Now, you've probably been warned about carbs in the past. It's true that they're not always beneficial. A fat, sugary doughnut is loaded with carbs, for sure—but it's the difference between simple and complex carbohydrates that counts. The good ones (complex) work through your system more slowly and have far better nutrients, rather than processed foods or refined sugar. We're all going to get our carbs, but it's important to choose those wisely.

Proteins. Amino acids are the key makeup of the proteins, and these are critical to the immune system. They can function as antibodies that keep us from catching the latest virus. Proteins aren't a direct source of energy in the way carbs are, but they're building blocks for other processes in our bodies. What's a "good" protein? It's measured in how many essential amino acids are within, and that's determined by what kind of food we're talking about.

When we think of proteins, we immediately think about meat and fish as strong sources of proteins. They contain those amino acids we need. But there are plant proteins as well. Vegetarians can get their proteins, though they need the right combination, because any particular plant protein alone usually lacks some of the amino acids we need.

Fats. Fats don't have the best reputation, but our problem isn't with fats themselves—it's with the saturated fats. What our bodies are looking for are unsaturated fats. These do a lot of good things: regulate our metabolism, keep our cell membranes elastic, help our blood flow, and promote cell growth. They also give us vitamins A, D, E, and K. So by all means, when you cut down on fats, make sure you're targeting the right ones.

Saturated fats provide us with cholesterol, which is tied in with hormone production. Cholesterol is another matter of poor publicity, but it performs a lot of positive functions in the body's system. And the right amount of cholesterol in our diet can reduce the risk of heart disease. To this end, please ensure regular blood tests with your family doctor to monitor cholesterol and your body chemistry levels.

Vitamins and Minerals. Most people recognize the importance of vitamins. We grew up with those cereal commercials that told us about our "minimum daily requirements" of the key vitamins. These and minerals make up the micronutrients. Our bodies don't need massive amounts of each, but they do need them. And we have to take some care in how we receive them. Vitamins can be broken down, for example, with cooking and heat, so those soft, heavily cooked green beans may not deliver the nutritional content after all. Minerals are sturdier—we can even receive them through the water and the soil in which the fruits or vegetables have grown.

Each vitamin has a "superpower" of its own. There are many of them, and we need them all. It's amazing how many different key functions they perform. This is another example of bringing nutritional information out into the light. Once we see the good things they're promoting in our bodies, we're motivated to eat better. Conversely, study the effects of unhealthy eating, and the "comfort food" of your imagination will quickly become discomforting.

Minerals are wonderful, too. They help your body balance its water content. They assist the work of the protein you take in, and they build healthy bones. They move the oxygen around in your body, which is vital, and they even help your senses of taste and smell. So the next time the aroma of rich coffee or your favorite baked dish gives you a happy moment, thank the minerals you've ingested that have enhanced your sense of smell.

BUILDING THE PERFECT MEAL

For a balanced diet, be sure you're getting the right portions from each of the categories below. Where are you already getting plenty of what you need? Where are you lacking? This book doesn't set out to offer detailed instructions for dietary practice, but to give you the basics and inspire you to take a deeper look.

CARBS: fruits; vegetables; whole grains including breads, pasta, and brown rice; sweet potatoes.

PROTEINS: meat, fish, eggs, nuts, seeds.

FATS: Avocados, salmon, mackerel, dairy products, nuts, eggs.

VITAMINS & MINERALS: Brussels sprouts, melons, berries, beans, spinach, kale, peas, potatoes, bell peppers, oats, chicken, mushroom, eggs.

CHANGING DESIRES

I had no particular motivation to eat the right things while I was growing up. I ate whatever was put in front of me, and I also ate the unhealthy stuff when I got a chance. Children and teenagers don't think too deeply about food. My first real food "aha moment" came when I read a book called *Body for Life* by Bill Phillips. I might never have picked it up if the title had been *Food for Life*, as one of the sequels is called. I was interested in fitness and building my muscles, and the author was a bodybuilder. But he spent a good bit of time talking about eating, and I'd never really thought much about food as a factor in bodybuilding.

The author had a lot to say about balance—carbs, proteins, and vegetables, as he divided them out. He gave easy-to-remember, common-sense advice about portion control (don't eat a baked potato bigger than your fist; vegetable servings should be twice the size of the others). That book left a mark; it gave me a plan that wasn't burdensome to follow. I found myself enjoying taking ownership over what I ate. I tried new things, such as a healthier salsa as a substitute for ketchup.

As I thought more about the value of what I was eating, I began substituting whole foods, real foods, and eating smaller portions but more frequent meals. Instead of eating a couple of heavy meals that made me want a nap, I'd have six smaller meals that boosted my energy. And I began to see sugar for what it is: one of the worst things we can put in our bodies.

My new diet allowed for a cheat day, too, and that gave me something to look forward to. If I could eat the right way for six days, I could eat whatever my heart desired on Saturday, my cheat day. Boy, was I going to have one colossal pizza—except, of course, when the time came, I didn't really want to overdo it. I was making too much progress! And my appetite had changed anyway. My stomach had a new idea of what was good for me and what constituted a tasty meal. And this, I found, was the real key: appetite. Change your desires and you can change your life. I was retraining an appetite for bad food into an appetite for what was good for me.

I was in my upper twenties, newly married, and my wife, Jennifer, and I enjoyed planning these meals together. There's tremendous power in the experience of having a partner in anything you set out to do. The two of us kept each other enthusiastic, and it was one more fun element to add to being married.

What I found was that the longer I stayed with it, the longer I created a pattern of eating right, the more the pattern became a habit, and eventually the habit became a lifestyle. For those struggling with this issue, those who are overwhelmed, consider this: I never had to face some ordeal of starvation or terrible-tasting meals. I never had to grit my teeth and depend upon sheer willpower so that one day I might have better eating habits. The whole thing was an adventure. At first it felt good, even victorious, finally to be eating the way I'd always known I should.

Once I realized the effect of food on my energy and efficiency in everyday life, I was motivated even more. There came a time when I had no desire to eat junk food. And that's the way I feel today. You'd have to drag me kicking and screaming from my eating habits. I still enjoy a cheeseburger or a pizza or a nice dessert (chocolate, please!); these things are now occasional and all the more enjoyable for it.

It might be the best lifestyle change I've ever made.

THE HYDRATION EQUATION

We need to talk about water, too. Are you drinking enough? I've never met anyone who didn't understand the importance of drinking enough water; after all, it's the most pressing requirement for survival on earth, next to breathing. But still, few of us drink as much of it as we really need. For one thing, we're addicted to soft drinks, coffee, sugary tea, and things that taste good. What we need, however, is water.

Why must we take in so much of it? What does it really do? Well, for one thing, water makes up 60 percent of your body weight.

If you weigh 180 pounds, more than one hundred pounds of you is H_2O! It makes you worry about evaporating into the air some night while you're sleeping, doesn't it?

That's not likely, because the fluid within is busy regulating our body temperature, lubricating our joints, preventing infections, and delivering nutrients to our cells. When our kidneys and our liver throw off dangerous toxins, it's because water is making that possible. There's a reason we could survive for weeks without food, but a lack of water would kill us within days. We need water that badly.

How much of it do we need? About a gallon a day (3.7 liters) for an adult male; about three quarters of that for an adult female. Does it have to be plain old water? No, it can come through other fluids that contain water, though things such as sugary sodas are much less helpful. A broth-based soup, tea, or even coffee can provide us with some of the water we need, and fresh fruits and vegetables are filled with water as well.

But a cool glass of water is the best of all. Dehydration from your body is happening all day in various ways. Don't drink your entire day's allotment of water, or even half of it, all at once. I've made that mistake, working through a session over Zoom and then realizing I didn't take a sip for the last ninety minutes. So I drank the entire water bottle at once. Neither is it a good idea to wait until you're thirsty, because thirst is just your body's way of telling you you're already dehydrated.

Just sip your water all day, keeping it flowing in small amounts your body can quickly use. Drink two glasses of water first thing in the morning, and one right before meals. Those are times when your body particularly needs a little fluid assistance. By the way, a big glass of water will also help you to cut down on your portions during the meal.

"Juicing" is popular these days, and fruit juice can have a lot of positive benefits in terms of vitamins and nutrition. But it can also contain a lot of sugar, and most of us need to be eliminating that rather than adding it.

Drinking more water is another easy boost for your health. You can even purchase a water bottle that keeps track of your refills and amounts during the day. For me, it's one more rewarding (and painless) discipline in caring for my body.

EATING FOR A PURPOSE

Everyone enjoys eating—as well we should. It's one of life's great pleasures. But it can be more than enjoyable. When we achieve optimal nutritional balance for our personal physical requirements, with the right macro- and micronutrients; when we're using the right habits, the right portions, and in the right timing; and when we pour plenty of water into the amazing machine that is our body—we become capable of far more achievement in life. We have greater energy in supply, our minds are clear and quick, and we actually enjoy our eating more rather than less.

In a society where overeating is rampant, we often fail to realize that nothing tastes as good anymore. We don't give our bodies time to work up an appetite before chowing down on yet another big meal. It feels good to work up an actual appetite. I might have craved a loaded pizza or a high-calorie dessert during that transitional time when I was building new habits. But those cravings pass, and after you overcome them a few times, they fade away. I look forward to my meals now, especially knowing I'm putting good fuel in the machine.

Remember also that all our essentials relate to one another. Good eating obviously helps the body and the mind. I would argue it's good for the soul, too. Relationships, too, prosper when we feel good because we eat right. What about financially? How much money do we spend on quick eating through eating out or a delivery service? Many people who begin working with financial planners are shocked to discover how much of their monthly budget is spent on dining out. It's one of the first lifestyle changes they make.

Which brings us to our next essential: money. How can we handle the challenge of our finances?

CHAPTER TEN

ESSENTIAL 5

MASTERING MONEY

"Wealth is the ability to fully experience life."

—HENRY DAVID THOREAU

Ken Jennings seemed like just another contestant on another TV game show. But by the time he'd been on a record seventy-four consecutive episodes of *Jeopardy!*, his was a household name in North America. Public interest in his winning streak boosted the show into a runaway hit, and eventually, with encore appearances and special events, he won nearly $4.5 million. At this writing, he has become one of the rotating hosts who replaced the late Alex Trebek on the show.

His arrival as a contestant, however, created a sensation. Over 182 calendar days, Jennings answered questions on an astounding array of subjects. You can't win on *Jeopardy!* without being well-versed in all fields from history to science to pop culture. But he came to realize there was one area where he needed to fill in some spaces in his accumulated knowledge: money. The Final Jeopardy! question that finally tripped him up was in the category of business and industry, and the answer that appeared was, "Most of this firm's 70,000 seasonal white-collaremployees work only four months a year." He offered, "What is FedEx?" But his opponent had the correct answer: "What is H&R Block?"

At this point, with his original streak at an end, Jennings had won more than $2 million, and it was time to figure out how to handle that much money. The general topic of taxes had defeated him, after all. So Jennings visited his local library—though you'd think he could have afforded to *buy* a book—and checked out a volume on how to avoid screwing up a financial bonanza.

"There are unbelievable statistics," he told the *New York Times,* "that three-quarters of all people who have some big windfall are out of money within two to five years. So many people are not smart about it. So I think it would be very ironic if I got the money for being smart and then did, like, something incredibly dumb with it."

Good point. Google "lottery winners who lost all their money" sometime, and you'll be astounded by the sheer number of people who won millions of dollars and watched it quickly slip through their fingers. Many of them, of course, go on mansion-and-sports-car buying sprees, and quickly become hooked on spending—or on narcotics, in one example. They fail to consider the tax angles and money management, spending above their means and ending up in debt. In one case, a man won the lottery, lost it all, *owed* vast sums, and took to robbing banks to pay it off!

Most of us are certain we'd do a much better job if we could only be handed a hundred million or so—and we'd certainly appreciate the opportunity to prove it! In most cases, however, money doesn't arrive in lottery winnings, signing multimillion-dollar NFL contracts, or attracting 250 million followers on Instagram. We actually have to put in years of hard work to earn that fortune. Then we must manage it wisely and cautiously.

Money is one of the most powerful forces in the world. It can do tremendous good or horrendous evil. It can feed countless starving people, or it can destroy a marriage. It can finance research to cure cancer, or it can buy weapons of mass destruction. It can multiply itself exponentially, if well-handled—or it can vanish in the flick of an eyelash. Money, like it or not, is an absolute essential in the journey toward fulfilling your true purpose.

MIND OVER MONEY

I've come to the realization that money is a relationship issue. Sure, it *affects* our human relationships; it can damage marriages and friendships, to be sure. It can also foster business relationships.

But I'm not talking about money and personal relationships; I'm talking about money *as* a relationship. How do we relate to it? In the previous chapter, we discussed food and realized that it's really a relationship, too. We need a healthy, rational way of relating to food based on our respect for its power and for our bodies' needs. Money may represent a different part of life, but again, we have an attitude toward it based on our history with it.

My life offers an example, just as yours probably does. I grew up in Toronto. My father was in real estate and was quite successful when I was young. During my earliest years, I was accustomed to large houses and swimming pools in the backyard. That was simply the view of life I was afforded upon starting out in life. Then, as can happen with real estate, my father fell from grace. Some of his projects and deals failed, and almost overnight, all the luxury disappeared around me. We were living in a subsidized apartment building on the other side of town. Our lifestyle completely changed, and as the child I was, it seemed unfair. You're pampered for so long, and then suddenly, it's all taken away.

I came out of that, as you can imagine, with a basic insecurity about money that I had to work through. At any moment, *poof!* It could all vanish. So I needed to make a lot of money and cling to it with all my strength. To this day, I'll check my stock portfolio with a distant trace of the old anxiety. Did I lose today? What if something happens to the economy again, and all that I have is gone overnight? Do I have enough? I'm learning to approach it differently, through my attitude and also my financial strategies.

My childlike view of money, of course, was unrealistic—luxury isn't an entitlement. But the anxiety that replaced that view wasn't healthy, either. When I was a younger man, financial insecurity had an impact on other parts of my life. Partners, clients, spouses, children—constant anxiety makes for poor relationships. We've all seen divorces that occurred in the midst of conflict over finances, and we've seen business partners with years of a friendship that ends in bitter dispute.

By now, you recognize one of the greater principles of this book: everything is interconnected when it comes to the essentials of life. Money matters create tremendous stress in life, which affects the body, the mind, and the soul. It hurts relationships. Even eating is interrelated with finance, because eating poorly is the route many take when facing anxiety. Perhaps of all our six essentials, money is the easiest to connect to the other five. That's because it touches everything in life.

For much of human history, this wasn't quite as true. It was possible to move through life with only a passing acquaintance with money or wealth. Today, seemingly, everything revolves around finance. It's all but required that we possess a credit card. Show me your checking account, or at least your credit card bill, and I can write a pretty accurate profile of your identity. Thus, much of our identity is tied to our spending. If we are what we eat, we are also what we spend.

MONEY'S TRUE VALUE

Money, then, is at the center of modern life, even if we have a contentious relationship with it. So we have to ask: what's the *true* value of money, beyond its exchange for the necessities we purchase?

Basically, it's this: money creates options. It allows *access to information*. It allows *access to people* and to *programs* that maximize our work and its reach. Financial resources give us the opportunity of gaining the information we need, knowing there are facts and realities we need to be aware of. For example, you wouldn't (successfully) invest in stocks unless you had a basic understanding of how the market works. That level of education carries a price.

We can also interact with the people we need, knowing there's very little we can accomplish alone. And it allows access to the programs we need, knowing there are systems, organizations, and processes that greatly increase our chances of being successful.

I'll offer a very simple example. I suffered a terrible back injury a few years ago. I had never known so much pain and discomfort could be possible. This was the kind of condition that totally derailed any work I might want to accomplish. I spent months under the care of a great chiropractor, and after that, not only did I recover, but I was able to thrive by taking my physical and mental capabilities to the next level. However, chiropractors don't volunteer their services. Most of us can afford a visit or two; few of us can afford month after month of weekly and twice-weekly visits. I needed access to that specialist. I needed information: which specialists could be trusted with my body? And I needed special treatments and programs—that helped me fully recover and even improve my condition.

I can attest that I didn't take any of that for granted. I often thought, "What if I couldn't afford this? What if I hadn't worked hard and invested carefully in the years leading up to my back problems? What would my options have been?" I shudder to consider it.

Access to funding affects all our essentials. In terms of food, there was a period of time when we were so busy, it was difficult to cook, so we found an almost cost-neutral way to have delicious meals that were also healthy. A personal chef came in on Sundays and prepared the next week's food for us, and because we needed fewer groceries and ate out less, the cost differential was actually very small. But would we have been able even to consider this without the financial blessings we had?

I've mentioned access to people as well, and I don't just mean the chiropractor or chef. I joined a group of peers in my field, an association of entrepreneurs. It gave me access to some of the greatest and most innovative minds in business. I wouldn't say the membership fee was inexpensive, but it was a fabulous investment in what I learned, and I've profited overall by my access to that information. It's been worth many times what it cost, but I still had to be able to afford that fee.

I've found that high achievers spend a lot of time working and accumulating money, but not enough time tending to what they've gained. In other words, another check has been deposited in our account. Should I just move on toward earning the next one, or should I think about how to multiply what I just received? If I bank it and forget it, what can go wrong?

Inflation, for one thing. Our money, left in a low-interest-bearing account, will be worth less tomorrow than it is today. That's just a basic economic reality.

Or consider business owners, who tend to feed most of their earnings back into their businesses, with little diversification outside of them. If something happens to the business, everything is gone. Consider a soup-and-salad restaurant that relied completely on diners making their own salads and helping themselves to soup and other dishes. It didn't weather the COVID pandemic, because even afterward, people have a different attitude toward a public salad bar and the health risks. I hope the owners had other investments.

There are also many people whose wealth is tied up in their primary residence. They bought the dream house after the agent encouraged them to stretch their finances rather than settling for their second choice. But real estate has its ups and downs. It's common financial practice to include the value of one's home in their net worth calculation. In my experience this is a mistake. A home should not be treated as an investment. It has utility and serves a function well beyond its financial components. When considering your net worth, retirement fund, and how much is enough for the future, leave your primary residence out of the equation.

MARRIED TO THE MONEY

As you've read this chapter, it's inevitable that you've thought about your own relationship with money. How are you and economics getting along?

It's a little like a marriage. Some people are highly incompatible with the whole subject of money. It seems that whatever they do, they can't get ahead, or get along. The money seems unfaithful; it always seems to be in love with someone else! There may appear to be irreconcilable differences between you and finance, but one thing is certain: divorce isn't happening. You two are yoked together forever, unless you want to relocate to an uncharted tropical island and live on fish and coconuts. The rest of us must live in a world regulated by financial transactions.

It's worth looking at those with positive, highly rewarding financial relationships as an example. Why does money seem to follow them like Canadians to hockey rinks? It's important to begin with personal reflection on the place of money in our lives. Assess your relationship:

→ Are you feeling good about the money you're earning and what happens to it after you earn it?
→ What about your current expenses? Do you feel they're manageable?

→ How about clarity? Do you feel like you're on top of your financial traffic, so that you have a firm grasp of income and outflow?

→ How much security or insecurity do you have about the future?

There are plenty of books on this subject, needless to say, and a lot of good ones. But general rules and concepts don't always help us. There are voices telling you how much you need for retirement, or what percentage of your income you should be reinvesting, but the truth is that every one of us has a different situation. In the end, we all have to manage our own finances, even if we hire professionals to help. We make the decisions.

So here are the three key issues at hand:

1. Discovering the truth about our relationship with money.
2. Deciding our level of satisfaction with our current financial situation.
3. Determining where we'd like to be financially in the future.

From there, we can talk about four principles that will always move us toward that destination. But first, we need to work through those three questions. You may well decide you have the money and the opportunities you need to maximize the six essentials and achieve your life purpose, all while living in a van down by the river. If that's true, Godspeed!

Or your situation could be the opposite. This is why I emphasize that everyone has a unique reality, and we each need to grapple with those three questions to come up with our own answers. Our theme is not how to become wealthy, but how to establish a healthy relationship with money.

These deliberations can be challenging for some people. Finance is a complex and emotional topic, but if we can't be honest with ourselves, we can't move forward. So this is one of those "put down the book moments," when you should take a break from reading and spend a few moments on reflection. (By the way, I'm not crazy about book reviews that say, "I couldn't put it down!" Reading is only taking in the raw material; reflection helps us integrate it into real life. So put the book down and think.)

After you've done that, we'll discuss the four fundamentals of our relationship to money.

INCOME AND EXPENSES

Income is just what it says: what comes in. Those with jobs receive payment, from which taxes are taken. There may be extra sources of income as well. Investments, interest from savings, rental from properties—money is generated. It's disposable cash, or at least fluid capital that could readily be spent. And businesses, like individuals, have income and pay taxes. The business owner decides how much to keep and how much to place back into the business. Growth-oriented entrepreneurs may take very little for themselves, choosing instead to prime the pump of the company as much as possible. These are all basic principles; money flows in, some flows back out.

We all decide how to parcel out our income. We have groceries to buy, a mortgage to pay, car payments, and then the nonnecessities that are still important for the enjoyment of life: eating out, vacations, entertainment, and all these things. Money is what makes it all possible. Many of us, I'm sure, could afford to spend much more time and thought on how that money is allocated.

The most basic truth of wealth creation is that, over time, income must exceed expenses. Over time, we won't make it very long with a widening trail of debt, which can become a vicious and inescapable cycle. Some people have no idea their typical monthly expenses exceed their income—or they'd rather not face the possibility of it. But it doesn't get any simpler than this directive:

INCOME > OUTFLOW

What comes in must exceed what goes out. As long as that's true, the difference is profit. And profit works over the course of time just as debt does, but in the opposite direction. It mounts up.

Grant Sabatier, a young college graduate, wanted some cash from the ATM so he could buy a burrito. He was disgusted to find just over two bucks in his account, and decided he was going to turn his finances around. At that moment, he was unemployed and lived with his parents. But he set a goal of making $1 million by age thirty. I imagine his friends had a good laugh.

Soon after, he found a marketing job and took on a few smaller gigs on the side. Using a little creativity and a lot of discipline, he found ways to bank half his income every week. He also bought every financial handbook he could find and diversified his money. He hit his goal by his thirtieth birthday, at which time he was a millionaire.

The importance of Sabatier's story is that he was an absolutely ordinary individual. He started with no advantage other than his education. But he had a very healthy and very *realistic* relationship with his money. He faced his poverty and set a new course. Notice how he followed each of the three initial steps: he got real about his money, decided he wasn't satisfied, and determined where he wanted to be. His course of action is available to everyone, as long as a profit stream is part of the equation.

A thoughtful budget is absolutely nonnegotiable. Simple spreadsheets can be drawn up to track all the monthly expenses, making sure it's accurate. The average earner should be able to set a modest goal of 10 percent profit per month. If she makes $4,000 per month after taxes, she should limit her spending to no more than $3,600—hopefully less than that. Important note: start from the monthly profit goal ($400, in this case) and work backwards. "Here's what we're going to save. Now, can we afford that weekend trip next month?"

The profit of $4,800 per year, invested wisely, will begin making money on itself immediately. As a matter of fact, many people will be inspired to say, "I think we can do a little better than that. Can we save 15 percent?" There are nearly always little expenditures here and there that can be cut, without making life austere and unpleasant.

For me, it's comforting to know my money is out working for me, every day.

> **ASSIGNMENT:** Create a simple spreadsheet showing all your known income on one side, all your expenses on the other. Be sure to budget entertainment, eating out, and any extras. Do you have at least 10 percent of your total income left over? Can you commit to save and invest that 10 percent profit each and every month? If not, what adjustments will make that possible?

ASSETS

If the difference between income and expenses is a positive number, we call it profit, and with it, we create assets.

This is where the real power of money enters the equation. Einstein is said to have declared that humanity's greatest invention is compound interest. Benjamin Franklin said, "Money makes money. And the money that money makes, makes money." It's actually harder to say than to understand! Because of compound interest, money can grow exponentially—not by simple addition but by multiplication, and then multiplication of the multiplication. Investment to maximize that kind of financial growth is a complex topic, but the purpose remains simple. Use profit to create more financial streams.

There are a handful of asset classes to be aware of—stocks, bonds, real estate, cash, and others. Getting a little bit more sophisticated, we also have private equity and other kinds of investing strategies to consider. Then there's speciality investments—investing in startup companies; collectibles, art, automobiles, stamps or coins, rare items; commodities, nonfungible tokens (NFT). It's possible to invest in anything that seems like a good bet to rise in value. All of that is to say there are various categories of assets that can lead to wealth accumulation.

Think again of the business owner who pours all his money into his business. It feels like the prudent thing to do, but to achieve diversification he must broaden his definition of (re)investment. He's missing out on a world of opportunity. During the last two decades, we've seen a bull run on Wall Street, significant stock growth beyond the predictions of most people. We also hear about a growing disparity in wealth, which is absolutely true. Part of that, however, is that the rich are getting richer as they've taken advantage of the new gold rush.

Diversification provides security. If we overload in one area—say, real estate—one crucial hit could be disastrous. Two things happen: first, we take a big hit to our net worth; second, we take a big hit to our self-confidence. The psychological impact of sudden loss isn't much different than what I experienced as a child, when large houses gave way to cramped apartments. Once bitten, twice shy.

Again, this isn't about Who Wants to Be a Millionaire. Plenty of other resources will help you with that. Our theme here is having a healthy relationship with the one great tool of access and buying power in this world. If you're overwhelmed, too busy, or unsure how to take control of your investments, find a qualified professional that carries a fiduciary responsibility when helping you. Let the buyer beware: there are profiteers out there less interested in helping you invest successfully than in their own commissions.

The Basic Math of Money

INCOME − EXPENSES = PROFIT

ASSETS − LIABILITIES = NET WORTH

LIABILITIES

Much like the relationship between income and expenses, we find that assets minus liabilities leads to growing our net worth.

Assets are anything of value we own. These could be stocks, our business, a house, or a document autographed by Abraham Lincoln. Imagine we have half a million dollars in assets. That's the total value of all our possessions. It's easy to see ourselves as worth half a million, but wait—while the house is worth $300,000, there's a $200,000 mortgage on it. So we must capture the mortgage owing as a liability. This means the house is a much smaller asset than we realized.

We may have loans, too. What about a car loan? Student loans? Credit card debt? Everything we're required to pay back is a liability. Here we have another concept so simple it's almost embarrassing to explain it. But people can miss the most obvious truths because money is an emotional issue if we're not completely honest, completely accurate in our assessment, and not completely healthy in our relationship with it.

We certainly want that assets figure to be a larger number than the one for liabilities. The hopeful part is that, over time, we should see the asset column grow, while managing our debt. We're paying down the house mortgage, we get the student loans paid off, and the car payment vanishes until we succumb to the temptation for another shiny new sports car. Knowing our assets and liabilities definitely makes us wiser in those decisions.

It's important for us to understand the time value of money, because not all debt is created equal. There's good debt and bad debt. Buying a house is definitely good debt. You're using and enjoying the house, and with any luck, it will rise in value. A loan for starting a new business is good debt, providing you execute on your business plan and you can service the loan. There should also be revenue from the business that helps to pay off the loan.

Debt actually has a value, if it gives us early access to something important. Few of us want to hold off on buying a home until we have all the cash to buy it outright.

But when we overextend ourselves, we learn about bad debt. That shiny new sports car is a good candidate for it. The debt is huge, and the car is devalued significantly the moment we drive it off the lot. And have we considered the service and upkeep on a high-level sports car? Bad debt is often a matter of borrowing from our future for pleasure today. That type of pleasure is fleeting.

Credit card debt is bad debt. The percentages of interest can approach 20 percent and become a trap some never escape.

Financial wisdom in a nutshell: make profit, create assets, build net worth.

TIPS AND TRICKS

It's very difficult to stop writing a chapter like this one. It could be two chapters, or two books, or a multivolume encyclopedia. We've kept things simple, because when we understand the basics really aren't complicated, we can build a healthy relationship with money and gain all the advantages that come with it. So I'd like to leave you with a few strategies I've found particularly important.

1. **Have an emergency fund.** Build it now instead of waiting. Six months of expenses will buy you a lot of peace of mind, as you know that any kind of income disruption won't knock you down. You'll have space to breathe, get your bearings, and figure out your next move.

2. **Get the appropriate insurance coverage.** For the same reasons as above, an ounce of prevention is always a wise course.

Home insurance, health insurance, or life insurance—whatever the area, we should never be so focused on business or profit that we don't take good precautions to plan for the unseen.

3. **Hire a professional accountant.** Avoid taxes. Read that again: I'm not saying to *evade* taxes. Every citizen has the responsibility to pay taxes to the government, but we're not required to pay the highest possible version of them. Not if there are legal ways to shield ourselves from that liability. The tax code constantly changes. A good accountant keeps up with those changes and will use them for your benefit.

Finances affect every part of life. If you can master the basics—not the advanced techniques of the world's leading stock traders, just the basics—and you can live from week to week with the discipline of a budget and a plan for the future, you can chart the course for your life purpose. It will also do wonders for your relationships, which happens to be our next and final essential.

CHAPTER ELEVEN

ESSENTIAL 6

STRENGTHENING RELATIONSHIPS

"Not for ourselves alone are we born."

—MARCUS TULLIUS CICERO

The name of Steve Jobs will feature prominently in twentieth-century histories of the business world. He was one of those very few people in history who changed the world, then went back to work and changed it again. As the CEO of Apple, he was one of the first visionaries to understand the full possibilities of a home computer. His company helped popularize, among many other things, the iPhone, which launched the smartphone revolution.

Jobs was a master business and marketing innovator. Like most inventors, he was associated with a few products that fizzled out, but the ones that did take off transformed the shape of daily life for hundreds of millions of people.

It's hard to think of anyone with more spectacular successes during the last fifty years or so. Yet before Jobs succumbed to pancreatic cancer in 2011, he told his interviewer, Walter Isaacson, that he harbored certain regrets. One was simply that he failed to combat his cancer more aggressively. He largely chose to ignore it, to believe that somehow if he just kept working, he would defeat the cancer through sheer willpower. Unfortunately, he had run into one obstacle he couldn't overcome through his own indomitable drive.

But it was the other regret that really caught my attention. Jobs called out his failure to be the kind of father he could have been. "I wanted my kids to know me," he told Jacobsen. "I wasn't always there for them, and I wanted them to know why and to understand what I did."

Isaacson's next question was whether Jobs was still glad he'd had kids. Jobs quickly replied, "It's ten thousand times better than anything I've ever done." Bigger, in other words, than the Macintosh. Or the iPod or the iPhone, all of which were worldwide difference-makers. His children, he now realized, were more important than any of those things. He had missed out on them, and of course, they had missed out on him.

US Congressman Paul Tsongas's observation has been repeated many times: "Nobody on their deathbed has ever said, 'I wish I'd spent more time at the office.'" Steve Jobs lived just long enough to affirm that truism. But I suggest the moral of the story is bigger than just spending more time with our families. It's about the long-term significance of *all* our important relationships.

Our spouses and children bring out some of the most basic elements of our true identity, and we change their worlds as well.

But a good, close friend brings out other important sides of us, and the impact there can be just as profound. Friends help us discover the activities we enjoy and share; they respond to and encourage the best facets of our personality. Similarly, work relationships bring out the portion of us that thrives on a shared vision, of joining forces to get something done. And through those relationships, we can accomplish big things.

Many parts of ourselves grow through our relationships, and in turn, make contributions to others. We need this growth to reach our potential—to fulfill our purpose to the fullest. In social context, you and I can become something greater than the sum of our individual identities.

Our sixth essential, then, is relationships. It's no coincidence that the other five lead up to this one; it's the culmination of them all. All our other essentials have been oriented to who we are as individuals—mentally, physically, spiritually—and in how we eat and how we spend. This final concept is how we take that person we've become and fit into society. How do we get along with people? How do we measure up as friends, as associates, as citizens, as children, as siblings, as parents, as spouses? Who is transformed due to our interactions, and vice versa?

Notice the range of relationships I've just listed. Life calls upon us not to relate to others in one kind of way, but in many. I'm a dad in a very different style than I'm a business coach, though there are similarities. I offer a different part of myself to being a husband than the part I offer to being a friend.

Are you a "people person," fluent in every relationship dialect? If so, you know just how to talk to a customer or a vendor, a good friend, or a grocery store cashier. In all these interactions, you're still yourself. You can be warm and encouraging, true to your values. But there are nuances to how you show up.

Some people aren't as socially adept. An invitation to a cocktail party or a meeting in the boss's office can range from nerve-racking to a simple annoyance. I've known brilliant business minds who struggle in the simplest dealings with other people. In fact, the biography of Steve Jobs tells the story of a brilliant outlier, an outside-the-box thinker who impacted humanity but fought with people. Some who worked with him described him as a "control freak," given to fits of rage and willing to humiliate his subordinates in public.

Some leaders are so gifted, they come to believe they don't need other people. But even the most brilliant leaders are, in fact, utterly dependent on others. And unless they're Steve Jobs–level incredible, they're unlikely to become leaders at all without good people skills.

Jobs or not, we need to be the best, the healthiest, the most well-rounded people we can be—mind, body, and soul—including in the arena of relationships. And whether you're a "people person" or not, you have the opportunity and the responsibility to maximize how you deal with all the key relationships in your life.

Think back one chapter. Our fifth essential concerned our relationship to money. I doubt anyone would challenge its position as a key factor in achieving our purpose. Finance is preeminent in all we do these days. But notice that one of the advantages we named in our chapter was that money gives us access *to people* and organizations. That is, money is a means to an end that is more important. Though some people behave as though people were the means and money were the objective, we know that the opposite is true.

The people in our lives are easy to take for granted, but they're the reason we're here. We tend to miss how important our relationships are not just to our social life or enjoyment, but to what we actually want to achieve in life. Friendship, marriage, and the rest—these are side considerations. We think they don't need real maintenance work. It doesn't occur to us to dedicate legitimate time and energy to stronger, healthier personal connections.

Life purpose, like all worthwhile things, is a team sport. It's not just a *you* thing, but an *us* thing. As a matter of fact, I've become a firm believer that success in life is adding value to other people. A genuine sense of purpose will ultimately point to something that makes the world a better place, so it becomes a question of service. In this chapter, you'll be challenged to examine your relationship skills, primarily in three key areas: personal, professional, and community.

> **THOUGHT EXERCISE:** If success in life is "adding value to other people," what does that mean for your current understanding of your purpose in life? What value do you see yourself adding, and to whom?

RELATING PERSONALLY

The first category of relationships has to do with our personal circle: family and friends. For most of us, these are the easy ones. Still, some "up close and personal" relationships come easier to us than others. I'm blessed to have found the most loving and supportive wife I could ever have asked for. Jennifer has been right there with me through the sometimes crazy arc of my career. It takes a special gift to be patient with an entrepreneur, and when I've sensed it was time for me to move in some new and crazy direction, she's been in my corner, always solid in support, always loving me and encouraging me every step of the way.

I have wonderful relationships with our kids, too, because I realized early on I had to make that a priority. If a marriage has "date nights," children deserve them, too. Time with each of them individually is key. Presence is the most basic expression of love, and I've worked to be there for them, to be involved in the issues they face, and to help them learn to make smart decisions. And as an example of the nuances of different relationships, I've had to figure out how to give to my kids. I want them to feel cherished; I want to give them gifts to make them happy. But I also want them to be well-grounded, disciplined, and clear on the fact that they can go out and earn things.

It hasn't all been easy. Early on in my marriage, I struggled with the concept of extended family. It wasn't something I experienced much, growing up. For me, family was defined as the people who lived under one roof. So once Jennifer and I were married, I figured out early on that in one sense, I was marrying a family—not just a woman. Her people were now my people. I was going to have to get used to regular Sunday night dinners with the in-laws. I loved my wife, and that meant learning to love those she loved. I had to put time and energy into that. In recent years, I've worked to become a better uncle and a better brother-in-law. That's not something I'd ever thought about in the past, but it's important to me now. I want to love and serve my extended family, and I know it makes me a better person when I do so.

As for friends, that word has been changed a bit by social media. I know people with thousands of "friends" on Facebook. Sometimes we have "friends" on that forum and we're not even sure who they are: Where do I know this person from? Did I just say yes to some anonymous friend request?

I don't mean that kind of friend—I mean the collection of people we have carefully curated, if you will, over time. We've maintained those friendships closely; we've nurtured them. It's been said we personally reflect the five closest friends we have. Later in this chapter, I'll ask you to try making a list of those and reflecting on what those friendships say about you. Together with our close families, good friends are our support and shield. They boost us when we need it and knock us back down when we need that too. We can think of them as our personal accountability team as we go through life.

So it stands to reason—if this is our team, shouldn't we review the roster every now and then? Shouldn't we think about each of these relationships and how healthy it is?

RELATING PROFESSIONALLY

There's another layer of relationships for us to navigate. Sometimes we choose a profession, and sometimes it chooses us. Many of us never intended to work in the area that ended up as our area. But whether we chose it or not, we most likely didn't get to choose our coworkers. Even a good CEO isn't going to build up an organization simply based on fun people to be around. Expertise counts. We all find ourselves working with bosses, subordinates, coworkers, clients, and vendors of all kinds. Their personalities may be grating. We may make a new best friend, or we may meet the worst person we've ever encountered—and there's a good chance we'll do both.

It doesn't take an amazing set of skills to be a good friend to someone you've chosen as a buddy. It does require attention to the basics of a good relationship, but most of us manage. We're good friends with people because we want to be. But relating well to people we're stuck with is the real defining feature of how good we are with people. Can you manage difficult relationships? Can you be a boss without abusing the power you hold in relationships? Can you work for a challenging boss without becoming bitter and counterproductive? Do you work well in team settings or on committees?

All those relationship basics apply here; it's the context that's different. Those around us aren't there for us to tolerate. They're there to help us (and for us to help) in building a powerful and effective organization. We need to maximize those relationships, even when it's difficult.

We make a lot of powerful and important friendships through the journey of business, and these are blessings we should cherish. They're also important responsibilities. I think of a close friend who went through a very rough period with his company. I happened to be very busy during that period; my own work was consuming me. Sometime later, I realized he had suffered, and I hadn't been there for him. He hadn't reached out, but he shouldn't have had to. I was negligent. As his friend, I'm called upon to serve, to heal, and to encourage. So I caught up with him and made things right.

That incident led me to doing some honest evaluation of how

good a friend I was in general. I now keep track of my communication with good friends, and I won't let time pass without checking in. I've found that, like the friend in my example, people won't always ask for help when they need it. But when they go silent, that may be their time of need.

I needed to be willing and available to serve. And my friend needed to be willing and available to be served. This is the essence of a relationship. We need *both*.

THOUGHT EXERCISE: Where do you excel? In serving or being served? Where can you improve?

RELATING IN THE COMMUNITY

Our three layers of relationships are like concentric circles. The first includes all those in our inner circle: our family and our close friends. These are our core relationships, near to the heart of our identity. Just outside that we have professional relationships, made up of those with whom we rub shoulders day by day, as we go about our business. These tend to be more assigned than chosen, and they require a little more intention and understanding as a result. And finally, we have an outer layer that's often neglected these days: community relationships. Through these, we touch the world that's outside the daily events of personal life.

We need to be involved with a community of some type, generally in the place where we live. This may or may not include churches, synagogues, mosques, or any other organized gathering places. We've discussed those in our essential based on the soul. But there are any number of other possibilities. There are business groups, peer groups, school associations, local governments, neighborhood associations, youth sports leagues, adult sports leagues, involvement in the arts, mission organizations, and the rest of the list would be all but infinite. The point is that the true sense of community is a bit harder to find today. We use social media to reach out, but it's a rather poor substitute for being in the room with other people and developing friendships.

There was a time before the internet, believe it or not, and a time even before television or radio. People were more likely to live in smaller towns once, and they took early evening strolls and socialized with their neighbors who sat on their front porches. Many folks attended the local high school football, basketball, or hockey games even with no children on the team; it was where people from around town met and caught up. This all may sound a little too nostalgic—so much whining over the "good old days"—but it's undeniable that we're more cloistered today. It's possible to spend all our time at home, at work, and in traffic, and to have almost no community footprint. As a result, communities suffer and we suffer. It may be that a public social gathering isn't your thing. And that's fine—just be sure to find what *is* your thing. What are your interests? Where do you have something to contribute?

Community involvement is an opportunity to expand our impact. Perhaps, if you serve as a volunteer board member of your local charity, there's no *direct* connection to your life purpose. But you'll have an opportunity to serve, to enrich the lives of others, and in so doing your own life will be enriched. Those with a large community footprint are surrounded by love and support. The people cherish them and come from every direction to show their respect.

By now, you're thinking about your own community involvement. Are you strong in this department, or is it something you've neglected? What are your areas of impact locally? What are some interests and skills you could contribute?

CAN YOU RELATE?

It's painful even now to revisit the memory, but not long ago, I lost my mom. She was in a hospice center at the end of a long battle with pancreatic cancer. She fought valiantly but just couldn't beat it. And at about five thirty in the morning, she passed out of this world. I was told there was nothing I could do, and that I should go home.

I thought about it, but here it was, the beginning of a new day, and what could I or should I do in such a moment? My grief was strong. I had a coaching meeting scheduled with a leadership team I was working with at the time. I was supposed to be there at eight thirty, and my first impression was that I should cancel; most people would. But I really didn't want to sit at home at this point. I wanted to do what I do, so I climbed into my car and went on to the meeting. When I got there, I did my coaching. But I was open and honest. I was able to share what had happened and what I was feeling, and the people in the room were a wonderful comfort to me. They surrounded me with support and love. I remember thinking, "Thank God I have this circle of friends, and that we can be transparent and strong for each other."

That group was a mixture of all the three groups I've discussed: friends, professional, and community. I'm grateful for relationships of all kinds. They add more to my life and my career than I could possibly explain. They've lifted me toward everything I've ever achieved, and even the confidence I needed to write this book.

I've mentioned that it's common for people to have about five key friends. It could be a little more, a little less, but we're limited in how many close friendships we can manage. What would your list look like? Earlier in the book, we talked about listing people we admire. As you list people who are your closest relationships this time, these two lists may overlap a bit. That's okay. But the focus now is to affirm who these individuals are, and then identify what the "glue" is in that friendship, because each strong, positive relationship tells us a little about ourselves. Why do we like these people? Also, why do we think they like us?

Next, you'll inevitably be led to thinking about your general skill level in relating to others. What are your strengths? What are your weaknesses? And finally, how do you see the importance of relationships in fulfilling your life purpose?

Aristotle said, "Wishing to be friends is quick work, but true friendship is a slowly ripening fruit." I think he nailed it. Relationships are work; they require time and energy. But the payoff is sweet indeed, and it bears seeds for the future. Good friends tend to lead us to other good friends, and in the end, we find we're no longer alone. We're part of a vast, powerful community of mutual support that reaches out both geographically and into the future. Relationships create legacy.

And that's where purpose comes in. Where do we go from here? What's a lifetime plan for building on all six of these essentials?

THOUGHT EXERCISE: Evaluate what you do well in relating to others, and what you wish you did better. Identify the important relationship in your life that needs the most work. How will you begin to do that?

CHAPTER TWELVE

STAYING ON TRACK

"An idea that is developed and put into action is more important than an idea that exists only as an idea."

—BUDDHA

Every new year is full of promise. What are your usual thoughts during the last, waning moments of a year? We might reflect on where we've been. Regrets? We have a few. But the people I coach tend to be forward thinkers. They like beginnings of all kinds—beginnings of opportunities, beginnings of businesses, beginnings of friendships. January 1 is a great title page for a book yet to be written.

That's not an original thought, of course. Have you ever driven by the local fitness center during the first week of the year? It's a little reminiscent of the department store the day after Thanksgiving. In other words, it's a madhouse. New members are signing up. Old members are rushing back into action, their clothes a little tighter. This is the year everyone is going to get on that exercise plan, start a new diet, and jump-start a life that's been idling in neutral.

How long does the New Year's surge last? Strava, an exercise tracking company, performed an in-depth study based on Google data and smartphone information. (As you know, human movements can be measured using the GPS information our phones put out.) Strava found that people begin giving up on their exercise kicks as soon as mid-January. The company specifically noted the third Thursday of January as the day when gym activities actually sink below the usual average.

Then Strava took a look at fast food consumption. You see where I'm going with this, don't you? After a two-to-three-week hiatus, fast food begins its early-year comeback. By forty days into the new year, people are munching burgers and avoiding the elliptical trainer just as they used to. I don't know how the Scottish feel about workouts, but they coined the proverb, "The best-laid plans of mice and men often go awry." Now we know exactly *when*—mid- to late January, apparently.

I doubt the typical reader of this book is a "plans awry" type, though. I'm betting you picked up this book because you're one of those people for whom the very idea of quitting, of giving up, makes you a little queasy.

High achievers are like that; they love the idea of perseverance and full accomplishment, tough as it is. *Surrender* is a dirty word. The question is, will they use the ideas in this book and take off and fly? Or will it be one more failure to launch, like all those easy formulas. And now that we've examined the six essentials for finding and fulfilling your purpose, what does that mean for the rest of your life? Are you likely to be excited about what you've read for a couple of weeks, and then move on to something else?

I hope not. I've written this book with a strong conviction that it offers something more lasting than a temporary high and a fast fade. Pursuing your life purpose is not a day trip; it's a lifelong journey. As a matter of fact, the road will take surprising turns. Your purpose will continue to grow and take on new forms, new nuances, new angles as you grow with it. Your goals will expand. Your vision will heighten. And finally, you'll be looking beyond the horizon to the next generation, and the legacy you leave to it.

This book's conclusion is your story's preface. The job hasn't gotten underway; you've only read the job description—and apparently, you're still interested in the work. So what lies ahead? How can you stay on track with the Six Essentials as a lifelong practice?

THE PURPOSE PLATFORM

Remember, we began with an exploration of how a lack of purpose leaves us open to the wrong drivers. Jealousy, guilt, resentment, fear, materialism, and a constant need for approval are some of the most common impulses that misdirect us into unhappy lives. And we concluded that the alternative was to be guided instead of driven. Guided by what? That's up to you. We spent a good bit of time together investigating what makes you who you are, because that's where we find the best clues to what you were made to do—that is, your life purpose.

From there, we spent six chapters of our twelve—the heart of the book—laying out the essentials of our identity. Nurturing and developing these—our mind, body, soul, nutrition, money, and relationships—creates a life capable of fulfilling that purpose to its highest potential. But it's more than obvious that none of that nurturing happens overnight. It's a lifelong education that never concludes. And that's a good thing, because it means there's always something more, something higher, something better for your life. The road goes on forever, and the journey only becomes more fulfilling.

This is why we used the imagery of the backpack. For a long journey, you take exactly what you need, and nothing more. You've given a good bit of thought to what should and shouldn't be in your backpack—the things in life that best define you and who you want to become. You haven't finished refining those contents, of course. The journey itself will change your ideas of what is truly nonnegotiable.

In this final chapter, then, we're thinking about the day-to-day itinerary for your journey; thinking about how to travel over the rest of your life. The Six Essentials are your guide rails along that road. As long as you develop and maintain them, and keep your eyes focused on your purpose, you won't go wrong. This is why I call this concept the Purpose Platform.

This book has been designed as a complement to other planning tools and systems because the people I coach tend to be motivated, and they already have a plan of some type. They're strategic about how they begin each new week, each new year. They don't stumble through time, but think through what they want to do, then move forward with full confidence. The beauty of what we're discussing here is that, if you already have a structure for your itinerary in life, the Purpose Platform works in accordance with that. It's designed so that anyone can add the concepts to whatever they're already doing.

We'll explore the path ahead based on understanding the framework, the process, and the journey.

THE FRAMEWORK

The Framework is already established: the Purpose Platform. The Six Essentials provide the blueprint for this journey and all you want to accomplish. But we're talking about much more than understanding what those six important elements of your life are. The key is to attend to all six of them without ignoring some and prioritizing others, as many of us do.

> **THOUGHT EXERCISE:** As you worked through the Six Essentials, which ones were you most comfortable in exploring? In other words, with which are you in the best shape right now? Which one was the least comfortable—the most ignored in your life? What do these two choices tell you about yourself? Try ranking the six, based on "needs the most attention" to "doing pretty well."

THE PROCESS

Through most of this book, we've thought and explored in the present tense. The question has been, who are you right now? At this point, we begin to think in the future tense. With each of these Six Essentials, what is your destination? Where would you like to be one or three or ten years from today?

Yes, I'm aware we live in a fast-paced world. Things change quickly; the entire landscape can be turned upside down overnight. For that reason, many people are unsure about setting long-term goals, and for good reason. We don't know what we don't know about the future. But again, the Six Essentials are crafted to withstand that uncertainty, because they're tied to things that don't change. You're going to have a mind, body, and soul no matter what. Nutrition will still be a factor no matter what crazy things happen in the economy, in the places we live, or in our families. We'll be spending some kind of money or other, and relationships will be with us as long as there *is* an "us."

It's imperative to set purpose-centric goals. Whether or not you strive to have a fully autonomous vehicle someday, or vacation in outer space with Elon Musk, you must think about what kind of person you want to be—in general and specifically, based upon your purpose and the essentials. Financially, you may want to be in position to own a certain kind of home. In terms of your body, you can set physical goals. There are goals for your marriage and family, for friendships. You could set mental goals in terms of education and reading plans.

To begin with, I recommend a three-year time frame for goal setting aligned to the Six Essentials. Three years is down the road, but not over the hill. Then, as you look at that three-year climb, you build the milestones working backwards—yearly, then monthly, then weekly, then daily. It's amazing how far you can go with just a little attention and checking in with yourself every day.

About those daily check-ins—take care not to let them be overwhelming. Remember, there likely are some of the essentials that won't need as much attention as others. I know people who are doing just fine in two or three of the essentials. Maybe they have a strong fitness regimen and a deep sense of spirituality played out in a religious setting or some other way. But they realize their nutrition and their relationships need work, or they're not developing their mind. So they apply a little more attention to the areas of need. How can they check in on the week's nutrition? Which day of the week would work? What about relationships and mental exercises? How and when?

Start with setting a handful of goals to accomplish over the next three years, then build the road to your ideal future taking yearly, weekly, and then daily steps.

> **SET THREE-YEAR GOALS.** For each of the Six Essentials, set an attainable goal, then break it down to reasonable milestones for the year, the month, and the week. Based on your ranking above, build out weekly or monthly checkpoints and place them on your regular schedule.

THE JOURNEY

You've heard the saying, "Nothing to it but to do it." On the contrary, I'd say there's a *lot* to it. It's not a matter of complexity but of durability. Will you commit yourself to creating your best life as a consistent process, day in, day out? Will you hold to that even when your life is disrupted and you find yourself in a new career or in the aftermath of a great setback?

Here's a saying I like better than the last one: "The problem with life is it's so...*daily*." If you could purchase the results of this plan from me, I'd be a billionaire many times over. Nearly everyone I know would pay a huge price to become the best, most purpose-guided person they can be. But I can't sell it to you. I can't do it for you. Only one person can. *You* must be the one to make the right moves tomorrow, then make them again the day after that.

Do this for a few weeks, and they become a habit. Keep that habit for a few months, and they become a lifestyle. Carry on a lifestyle for a few years, and it becomes an identity. At that point, less willpower is needed. After all, it takes minimal discipline to brush your teeth each day. It became a habit long ago, then just a part of your day you don't even think about.

Wouldn't it be nice to make all the right moves in these Six Essentials with the reflexive daily rhythm of brushing your teeth, so that you can't imagine going a day without caring for all the elements that make you better?

It can be done, just not by me. What I *can* do, however, is give you a snapshot of what this lifestyle looks like for me. Being guided by my purpose and tending to the Six Essentials have already become ingrained in my life, and I can't imagine any other way. I'm often asked about my routine, and I find that people enjoy seeing a template for the Six Essentials + Purpose lifestyle, even if it's not the exact template that will fit their life. Here's how I navigate my journey.

A DAY IN THE LIFE

Right now, I am an Expert EOS Implementer™. I coach and help entrepreneurial leadership teams achieve their organization's goals. My three-year plan isn't going to be drastically different from that, but as I focus on my purpose I am being guided to help those leaders achieve their personal goals as well.

Presently I have a three-month goal of making online tools available for the readers of this book, to help them use technology to follow their purpose and the Six Essentials. But goals should be thoughtful. I won't just consider the technology angle, but the Six Essentials as well. In order for me to develop the best possible solution, I must be "firing" on all Six Essentials. I will require my mind, body, soul, nutrition, money, and relationships to be in the best possible shape they can be. There's a reason we noticed, all through the book, how these essentials overlap and actually work together to help us achieve our goals.

As a matter of fact, if I have a "soul goal" and it has to do with reflection or meditation of some kind, it might be that I can accomplish that while running. That's a great time for reflection, prayer, or mindfulness.

These are general examples of how I might think of goals and use my schedule and the Six Essentials + Purpose to help me get there. But I've become much more organized about my schedule. It's all written down so I can check it frequently. Here's how the actual schedule looks:

Starting the day: Notice during the following that I address the essentials before I do anything else that day. If I leave these things for last, it's too late. I'm girding myself with these best practices before the day's work even begins. That helps to reinforce to me the high priority of working each day toward becoming my best self and fulfilling my purpose.

I usually rise at six. I'll walk outside perhaps for ten minutes (it could be more) so I can go ahead and get some daylight into my system. I've learned that it's important for the body, producing vitamin D, supporting bone health, and lowering blood pressure. It's also healthy emotionally and is nature's caffeine.

Journaling. Then I spend time journaling. That, too, follows a system. I'm specific about checking on where I am with all six Essentials. I even give them one-to-ten grades. I also look at the day before in my journal. How did I do? Well, perhaps I fell off on nutrition. If so, I'll redouble my efforts to eat right today. This is the best time to think about that.

I also include "First Thoughts"—literally the first thoughts I had during the walk. This is about creating an opening for thinking outside the box, so all this doesn't become too mechanical. I'm open to new ideas and creativity, and I also identify and add something I am thankful for.

Serendipity Moment. There are no coincidences. This I believe. The trick is to pay attention to yesterday's interactions, encounters, and events. There is always something to highlight that confirms I'm on the right path, making the best decisions possible.

Daily Intention. I will list out in point form the important events that will make up a successful day. For example, if I have a coaching session that day, my intention will include facilitating to bring out the best in my clients that results in a 10 out of 10 session rating.

Soul Time. Then I have time devoted to the soul, based on my particular faith. This is generally a reading and a time, in my case, for prayer. As always, you'll personalize your approach.

Professional Growth. I also set out a time for reading within my field of business and interests. This works toward some of my mental goals. This does not include the news (often a distraction), but intentionally taking in new information geared to what I do or what I'm interested in at the moment.

Meditation. After that, I'll spend time in meditation, for usually ten to twenty minutes. We've already discussed meditation in an earlier chapter. It's a time to step aside from life and distractions to allow the mind to rest and rejuvenate.

Clearing the Deck. Only at this point will I attend to work items (emails, voice mails, etc.), and just to take a broad survey of everything I've got going on, just to make sure there aren't fires to put out or items of immediacy.

Workout. Exercise time can vary. An hour is optimal, but there are days when I only have time for thirty minutes. The workout, too, has a weekly schedule of whether I'm attending to strength, cardio, mobility, or something else.

Meals. There's time in there, of course, for a healthy breakfast. I've been making sure I'm disciplined about that, too, and not just waiting for lunch. I call all this my "Morning 90," because it averages ninety minutes. If there's time left over, I can work. But by the time I do take on my workday, I've conditioned my mind in a number of ways. I'm thinking in a healthy way. I've already given attention to all the essentials. Mentally, physically, and emotionally, I'm ready for those prime hours when I'm most alert and productive.

Segments. I've learned, from my own experience, that we have limits to our best attention span. During the day, I try to break my focus time into ninety-minute increments. If I have a coaching session, if at all possible I take a fifteen-minute break every ninety minutes. We simply won't be at our best over longer stretches.

Other Meals. I may not have precise plans for lunch and dinner, but I have guidelines. A heavy carb-loaded lunch is going to damage my energy and focus in the afternoon. I can add more complex carbs or starches at dinner, since those actually help us sleep. Elsewhere in the book, I've given some of my thoughts about getting the best sleep. It's so important that we maximize our rest period, and what, how, and when we eat can help with that.

For me, an optimal day is being up at six, asleep at ten—eight hours of rest with sixteen hours used as productively and wisely as possible. I hear a lot of talk about how little time we have; you can accomplish your life's purpose one hour at a time.

And when I go to bed at night, my last thoughts are always positive, grateful ones. Think about the nice kind of tiredness you experience after a productive day. The bed feels good, my mind is at peace, and I drift off to sleep, ready for the next round.

> **CREATE A TENTATIVE MORNING PLAN.** What would an ideal daily startup look like for you? What elements should you include as you start your day? Then, when you have a good idea of what it would look like, try it out for one week and adjust as needed.

STARTING HERE, STARTING NOW

We began this book with the idea of chasing squirrels—the well-observed phenomenon of people who live a cluttered life of brief distractions, scattered priorities, and frustration, more and more driven by impulses and emotions that could ultimately make them miserable. Contrast that with the life we've sketched out here: intentional, meaningful, with a view toward the future but a plan for the moment. Where have these chapters brought your thinking? Are you closer to identifying your purpose? Have you removed a few items from your backpack and added others? Which essentials need the most immediate attention in your life?

I want to hear from you along your journey. After all, you're not traveling alone. Our journeys may look a little different, and may have varying destinations, but we walk together. We share ourselves. We laugh and cry together, offering a pat on the back when it's needed, or a kick in the rear when that's needed instead. We discover a great exercise or nutritional concept, and we share it with each other.

So the final tool I offer you comes from the relationship essential. Share your journey with others. Visit our website at www.tedbradshaw.com and take advantage of the tools offered and the traveling companions you'll meet. I don't know about you, but traveling with a friend is much more fun for me than traveling solo. Let's make this journey a convoy.

Lao Tsu said, "A journey of a thousand miles begins with a single step." That's been the idea for this chapter, the guiding principle behind this book, and the imperative for your own journey toward purpose and impact. One step. Then another. No looking back.

What's your next step?